W9-BIW-385

Lyrical Laps and Laughs

2007 NASCAR Nextel Cup Points Race Re-Caps

... From a Jeff Gordon Fan's Perspective

Maria Bennett

The Original Route 66, Inc.
Publishing Division
www.TheOriginalRoute66.com

LYRICAL LAPS AND LAUGHS

Published by The Original Route 66, Inc.
Publishing division
©2007 by Maria Bennett

FOR INFORMATION:
The Original Route 66, Inc.
P.O. Box 223057
West Palm Beach, FL 33422

www.TheOriginalRoute66.com

Manufactured in the United States of America
First Edition/ First Printing

Library of Congress Cataloging-in-Publication Data: pending

ISBN 978-0-9799934-0-4

~It is better to be hated for what you are,
than to be loved for what you are not.~

CONTENTS

FOREWORD

NASCAR Nextel Cup Racing . . . *and poetry*. Okay, *there's* a combination you don't hear of often. And at first glance it might seem about as welcome as mustard on a doughnut, but Maria Bennett has a way of re-capping a weekly NASCAR event in prose that makes the readers feel like they are at the race track themselves. Maria has long been a Jeff Gordon fan and has taken her love of motor sports and writing to a new form of expression for race fans. What first drew me to Maria's writing was her absolute demand for historical accuracy. Each week she takes us back to a week in review in Nextel Cup competition and does it all with a lyrical and humorous style that, well . . . almost makes us race fans forget were reading poetry! Every race is looked at with an eye to accuracy in terms of events and outcome, and even though she writes from the perspective of a Jeff Gordon fan, anyone can gain insightful knowledge of the preceding week's race by reading her words. Her style is unique and unlike anything that I have come by in the past.

In my 15½ years of hosting *For Race Fans Only* on QVC and a lifetime of being a fan of all types of motor sports, I have read just about every form of race report. I spend almost 20 hours a week reading and re-reading sports pages, news releases, publications and newspaper clippings. I have found Maria's weekly re-caps to be a fresh and entertaining departure from the mundane and look forward to making her writings part of my weekly prep for the show.

I encourage you as a Jeff Gordon supporter, or just a race fan at heart, to sit back, relax and be taken back through the 2007 Nextel Cup season in a way that only one writer has chosen to take us. *Poetry* . . . and *NASCAR* . . . hand me another doughnut with condiments on it!

Dan Hughes,
Host of QVC's *For Race Fans Only*

ACKNOWLEDGMENTS

Thank you to my **Lord and Savior, Jesus Christ** for creating me with a love for racing, and for giving me the ability, strength, and a little bit of talent to write about it! May you, ultimately be honored above all else!
"Racing is my thing, but Jesus is my King!"

Thank you to **Mom and Dad** for your never-ending constant love, support, and encouragement, and for always sharing in my hopes and dreams! And for sharing in the love we have for our favorite driver!

Thank you to my **precious husband, Marty**, for putting up with your crazy wife and yet another one of my endeavors! Thank you also for your computer wizardry! So many things I couldn't do without you! And thank you for loving racing *almost* as much as I do! And thank you for loving me.

Thank you to my **precious son Anthony**! You'll never know how much it means to have you look forward to my weekly re-caps! Your support and positive comments mean the world to me! I love you more than words can say!

Acknowledgments

Thank you to **Mom and Dad Bennett** for your encouragement along this journey, and for always printing out my re-caps and forcing anyone who will, to read them! Your love and support is a blessing!

Thank you, **Dot** for cramming a year's worth of work into a couple of months! I have learned so much from you! It is an absolute joy and hysteria-filled pleasure to work with you, and learn just how a bunch of words and a vision can actually become a real book!

Thank you to all of my faithful readers and fellow Jeff Gordon fans on the **Jeff Gordon Network**! Your unfailing words of encouragement are what kept me going! You guys are the absolute best!

A big thank-you to **Debbie** for being the *World's Greatest Go-Between!* Thank you for delivering my re-caps to John every week! I am blessed more than you know by your sweet spirit and helpful attitude.

Another big thank you to **John Bickford**! As you can see, your suggestion to turn my weekly re-caps into a book has gone a long way! I have gleaned much from your knowledge and grown as a person because of it, and because you believed in me. Thank you for enjoying my words and music and for being so kind and encouraging to me. It's easy to see where Jeff gets his class!

And to **Jeff Gordon**. I know you know your friends, family and fans love you, but I doubt you will ever know just how much! Without you, NASCAR would never be the sport that it is today. For that, we thank you!

INTRODUCTION

with "The Off Season Blues"

I don't know if you've noticed yet, but I happen to love NASCAR! The sport is under my skin, and resides within the nucleus of every cell and fiber of my being! I don't even know why, but I love every detail about it! I want to know all I can about how the racecar is set up for race day, and what kind of adjustments need to be made throughout the race. . . . **However**, I could care less about our family car! I'm not even sure how to jump start the thing! I do know where to put the gas and how to drive it, but that's about as far as my interest level goes. But everything relating to a stock car and stock car racing holds my interest! *What's the deal?* **What's wrong with me?**

- I want to know the details of every track.
- How many degrees of banking does it have, and how does it vary in each corner?
- What's the surface made out of?
- How long is it?
- Are we starting with scuff tires or stickers?
- How much horsepower was on the *dino* reading?

···

I love the noise of those awesome machines careening around the track! And I would give my right arm, before I die, to be given the opportunity to do a burn out and envelope the entire car in smoke until the tires are shredded! *And I'm a girl! I mean, a real "girly girl!"* I love to watch all the pre-race coverage! I love the F-16's or whatever aircraft happens to do a fly-over on race day!

I love to hear the National Anthem! I've been singing our National Anthem for years, and have sung for countless professional sporting events, but trying to get the opportunity to sing for a Cup race, well . . . apparently it takes an act of Congress! One of these days . . . Preferably *before* I am committed to a nursing home! (Or insane asylum, whichever comes first!)

Well, in case you haven't figured it out yet, Jeff Gordon is my driver! I am about as devoted a fan as he'll ever have! I'm not the star-struck stalker type, however! After all, he is a human being. I feel more like a proud sister, if that makes any sense! I first had the opportunity to meet Jeff when my husband and I were asked to work at his Charlotte fan club event in 2003. His then fan club director invited me to sing a Patriotic mini-concert at his Daytona fan club event the following February! (Thanks, Carol!)

I really don't know what inspired me to write these lyrical-style re-caps. I guess it began when I wrote a little poem that you will find at the end of this book, and it made me think, *Hey, wouldn't it be cool to re-cap a whole race this way!* I was tired of the same, boring old race re-caps week after week. I wanted something that was not only historically accurate, and a genuine race re-cap, but funny and entertaining as well. And, being from a Jeff Gordon fan's perspective makes it all the more unique! So I started writing these things, just for fun, and posting them on the Jeff Gordon Network Forum. The response was overwhelming, and people continued to ask if I could do it every week.

I hope as you re-live the 2007 NASCAR NEXTEL Cup season, my writings will jar your memory of some of the finest moments in NASCAR history! I hope some of the funny, or even stupid lines will bring a smile to your face for years to come! And if you happen to be a Jeff Gordon fan, I know you will enjoy re-reading about his many record-breaking accomplishments from this incredible year, and continue cheering on, in my humble opinion, the greatest driver that ever walked the planet! He has gifts that only our Great Creator could instill! I am so glad He did! And, for some reason, He also allowed me to catch this *NASCAR disease!* And if you know of a cure . . .

I'm not interested!

THE OFF SEASON BLUES
by Maria Bennett
©2005

The banquet is over,
This crazy season is done,

The wait for Daytona is now a long one!
I'm glad for the rest that our Jeff can receive
Along with the team and his tired crew chief, Steve!

Yes, they need a break, but I CERTAINLY DO NOT!
Several weeks without NASCAR is not what I want!

But you can't change the holidays
Or that special time of year,

When the whole entire world
Seems to be filled with good cheer!

"Everybody likes to take a holiday," I sing;
"Everybody needs to take a rest."

But I've asked a few 24-fans I know,
And we don't need a break from rootin' for our Jeff!

So to help us cope in this terrible drought,
The gifts we buy loved ones will have 24's all about!

There'll be 24-stockings filled with 24-stuff,
Chocolate 24 racecars, calendars, and such!

A cool flame car tin with little 24-mints!
——Items galore on our 24-wish list!

Santa even remembers my little dog somehow,
With a new 24-dog dish to hold her little-dog chow!

But amidst my depression in this "No NASCAR Season,"
It's not hard to reflect on the holiday's *true* reason!

So much to be thankful for,
The blessings abound,
Reminders in the songs that are sung all around!

Although one Christmas song seems to be stuck in my head,
One with new words than what the original said!

I'm sure Elvis never meant for his song to be about,
Sad Gordon fans and the racing we were without!

But here goes nothing; Now I'll sing it for you,
I'm sure you'll relate, if you're a true fan that's blue . . .

The *New* Blue Christmas
by Maria Bennett
(Sing to the tune of *Blue Christmas*, by Elvis Presley)

Jeff,
We'll have a blue Christmas without you,
We'll be so blue thinkin' about you.

Lights glowing red, on our green Christmas tree,
Are reminders of flames,
That are not here with me!

We have some J. Gordon ornaments, that's certain,
But their reminder makes our blue heartache start hurtin'!

Introduction

But those snowflakes of white,
Give us hope and some light . . .

They brought the noise I just heard,
It was the snowplow in the night!

You see, when I hear that snowplow's big engine,
It reminds me of 800 horsepower's revvin'!

And I know with that sound,
Soon Daytona will come around!

And soon 'twill be time,
To cheer Jeff on to "Number 5!"

So when your blue heartache starts hurtin',
And when the New Year rings in, know for certain,

You'll be doin' all right,
A new season's in sight!

You'll forget,
'Bout your blue, blue, blue, blue Christmas!

CHAPTER 1

Daytona 500
Daytona International Speedway

February 18, 2007

Nothing like counting down the days for three months for racing season to begin, the day after it ends! We are NASCAR fans. That's what we do! Obsessed? Maybe. Slightly crazed? Definitely! And if you claim to be a Jeff Gordon fan, you had better be! None of this, "I think I'll root for 'so and so' this week if Jeff isn't running well" stuff! That is NOT a true, dedicated Jeff Gordon fan! Statements like that irritate me to no end! Maybe it's my nature. I'm a dedicated type of person. Dedicated to my husband and family, dedicated to my God, dedicated to whatever work project I may be doing currently (which usually is a lot of things!) And yes, 100% dedicated to my driver! My driver is Jeff Gordon. Through thick or thin, good times or bad, it doesn't change a thing! The Daytona 500 is here! All I can say is, "it's about time!" Woo Hoo! The 2007 season has begun! Last year, my husband got us Daytona 500 tickets for Valentine's Day! What an experience! It was a blast, even though I truly thought I would freeze to absolute death! I am originally from upstate New York, and trust me, up there, they get winter! However, all the years I lived up north, I truly don't think I have ever been as frozen-to-the-

*bone cold as I was at the 2006 Daytona 500! It was a day unlike any other that I had experienced in almost 23 years of living in south Florida! We drove up to the DI Speedway that morning, and were at the track from early morning until after the race that night. The HIGH for the entire day was only about 53 or 54 degrees, which isn't that bad, but it was a cloudy, windy day, with an icy mist in the air that blew straight through to my bone marrow! Being that we were outside in it almost the entire day, it was easy for our bodies to cool down to corpse-like cold by the time the race began, and, the temps dropped down to the 30's mid-race! Not to mention, we were sitting on metal bleachers! I felt like I was naked, sitting in a snow bank for hours! My teeth literally chattered the entire time, and I could barely talk! (Let's just say, I **DO NOT** see an Alaskan vacation in my future anytime soon!) **HOWEVER**, I'd do it all again in a heartbeat! When 43 800-horsepower engines come screaming around the corner at you, let me tell you, your blood will boil no matter how much hypothermia has set in! If you ever have an opportunity to go to the Daytona 500, GO! Rent a NASCAR NEXTEL FAN VIEW device (those things are cool!) and soak in every minute detail of the experience you can! Even if you almost sacrifice your life in the process,*
Trust me, it will be worth it!

A pre-spring storm is brewing!
It's been festering for a month!

NASCAR fans are quickly jarred
From their off-season, hibernating slump!

The imposing tempest has been blowing since Testing——
——That January *tease!*

But no need to batten down any hatch,
So put your mind at ease!

Daytona 500

There's plenty of thunderous rumble!
Chill and heat both fill the air!

The teams and haulers are raining in!
With shock and awe, we simply stare!

Thousands chase this impending storm!
To where it all begins!

The biggest, blustery tornado around,
You'll ever want to reside within!

The hallowed gates of Daytona!
Are finally blown open today!

It's "kick off" time at DIS,
NASCAR's Super Bowl is underway!

The off-season blues have plundered!
The boys are back and ready!

Time now again, for the 49th running,
Of our spine-tingling Daytona 500!

The air is thick with electricity!
People scurrying here and there!

Everyone clad in their favorite driver-garb,
Festivities everywhere!

Though the air is quite chilly and blustery today,
No one really seems to notice!

To see the first race of the season live and in person
Is an extra special bonus!

Who cares if you have to *pay through the nose*,
Just for a place to park!

We don't even notice that our seats are miles away,
Or that the wind's bite is worse than its bark!

After the Qualifying races, (Jeff won his!)
The scandals are already starting! *Let the games begin!*

The 9, The 17, Riggs, Sadler and Waltrip,
Are all racing without their crew chiefs today!

Their post-race inspections failed to pass,
Talk about attention-getting media display!

Jeff's car failed too,
But not for cheating reasons!

Deemed *unintentional* for them,
By those officials that are seasoned!

But he must start 42nd!
Way in the back!

His winning-position from the Duel
Was disallowed just like that!

So many changes, before the GREEN ever waves!
——From the new Toyota car, to the changes in the Chase!

——This year there will be 12 who will race for the Cup,
And points added for wins, which should provide extra spunk!

The Earnhardt family feud is under the scope!
Will Jr. stay or leave? No one really knows!

Daytona 500

We are also reminded to remember
Those special ones who've passed——

Bobby Hamilton and **Benny** Parsons,
And the times they made us laugh!

Their families are in our thoughts and prayers,
Our hearts go out to them!

May their fond memories of happier times,
Never, ever end!

As 98 countries are now tuning in,
"Since You've Been Gone" is being sung by Kelly Clarkson!

"Big and Rich" sing our Anthem
Those F-15's are awesomely loud!

That giant American flag being displayed,
Makes me amply, extremely proud!

The moment we've been waiting for,
All winter long!

So much has happened right,
But so much could still go wrong!

Come on Jeff! You're a Pro at this place!
To win from 42ⁿᵈ, for you is a *piece of cake!*

David Gilliland leads the entourage,
Of colorful, spit-shined machines!

You boys have 200 laps,
To race each other clean!

"Boogity, boogity, boogity, let's go racing!"
Was D.W.'s screech!

Gilliland led lap 1,
By lap 2, they're "cheek to cheek!"

The 24 is on the move!
By lap 4 he's accelerated up 8!

Lap 10 he's up to 25th!
He's looking good right out of the gate!

Jeff scrapes the wall ever so slightly,
On "unlucky" lap 13!

After the first CAUTION on lap 16,
Kurt Busch steals Gilliland's lead!

By lap 34, it's Tony Stewart,
Assaulting Busch for first!

Stewart's never won the Daytona 500,
So if you're in front of him today, you're cursed!

The second YELLOW of the day is on lap 80,
And boy, was it crazy in the Pits!

Not sure if I can write all the action in a couple of lines,
But I'll try and make it fit!

First, the Caution was for Kyle Petty's right rear,
It let go and dropped *tons* of metal debris!

Metal and tires is a really bad mix!
To figure this out, doesn't take many brain cells, you see!

Daytona 500

Stewart stalled on pit road,
Then a wreck happened,
Right in front of his face!

Robby Gordon and Gilliland kind of collided.
The 7 was exiting and ran out of space!

Tony's bad luck continued,
He was too fast exiting the Pits!

He was sent to the tail end of the longest line,
Restarting 40th instead of first gave him fits!

Not only that, he noticed his oil pressure dropping,
While pacing slowly under the Caution!

Hmmm, the plot thickens, will he win this race?
Right now, it looks like he's lost it!

Lap 90, who's in tenth?
Looks like our 24-gent!
Obviously he's been cruisin' for sure!

That first spot is calling out to his name,
Who can avoid its lure?!

There was **almost** a huge wreck,
Just after halfway,

Stremme **almost** got turned by Harvick,
Who was up in position eight!

It could have been messy!
Everyone checked up!

My heart almost stopped,
And I had to re-swallow my lunch!

Well, by lap 122, Jeff's Goodyears were spent!
His "get up and go," got up and went!

He was in 34th when finally GREEN stops began!
Come on 24-team, help him if you can!

The 31's jack man popped a calf muscle!
Not only is that gross, it will bankrupt your hustle!

With 58 laps to go,
Stewart's climbed back to **fifth!**

Even though Jeff's the fastest Dominoes Hot-Lap car,
He's in 28th really needing a lift!

Busch and Stewart are back at it on 149,
Stewart leads with 50 to go, and then . . .
Oh my!

There's a big crash in turn 4!
Can you guess who was in it?
Tony got loose and Kurt sent him spinnin'!

Stewart's 9th attempt to win The 500 today,
Will come up short, once again,
Due to this on-track display!

On lap 162,
The 24's in nineteenth,

The top 20 cars are within one second of each other,
And run 3-wide and way deep!

Daytona 500

Jeff makes it 4-wide on 166!
Not sure if I can hold my breath for 33 more laps of this!

27 laps to go, when a big *disruption* occurs!
This CAUTION involves The 48, who "just lost it," so I heard!

Four other cars pretty much sealed up their fate!
Thank goodness Jeff got by with a narrow escape!

With only 9 laps to go, Jeff's in twenty-third!
Will his first race of the season end just shy of absurd?

Well *pull your belts tight!* Hang on for dear life!
Right now the real action begins here tonight!

With 8 laps to go,
Kevin Harvick's in fifteenth!

Kyle Busch got Mark Martin loose,
But both are still going for the lead!

Jeff's in eighteenth with only 6 laps to go!
Everyone's *turning up the wick* at the end of this show!

Five more to run, when the CAUTION flag flies,
The 17's in the back of McMurray, collecting four other guys!

Dale Jr.'s in the mix, along with McMurray and The 88,
The 1 of Martin Truex is the last one to "skate!"

The RED flag is thrown with only 3 laps to go!
It will be a GREEN/WHITE checker finish,
Don't even think about leaving this show!

Jeff is up to twelfth when we go back to GREEN,
The 5's all over Mark Martin's bumper,
Who's running in the lead!

Will Mark get his first Daytona 500 win,
After trying for so many years?

Suddenly the crowd goes wild!
For this *legend*, everyone cheers!

With 1 lap to go, who's this sneaking on the outside?!
Where in the world did Harvick come from?!

Now he's right up to Martin's right side!
He got him loose and in a blink, **it's Harvick that won!**

Well the excitement doesn't end there,
The *Big One* happened just before the finish line!

There are wadded up cars, smoke and fire,
But thankfully everyone's fine!

Jeff was in the melee, but ended up tenth!
Considering today's trials, it's not a bad way to end!

Mark Martin came up short
By only .002 of a second!

But with his incredible positive attitude,
We all could learn a lesson!

And so begins the season!
We're *off to the races, my friends!*

Daytona 500

Will this be the year our Jeff takes the Cup?
I can't wait to see how it all ends!

But lets keep our focus,
It's now *California or Bust!*

Where Jeff and Team 24 will be amazing,
On this you surely can trust!

CHAPTER 2

Auto Club 500
California Speedway

February 25, 2007

Isn't February just such a great month?! Well, I guess not for everyone, but it's one of my favorites! Besides the obvious . . . **THE BEGINNING OF RACING SEASON! (Hello!)** *It's a very festive month in the Bennett household! My husband's birthday is at the beginning of the month, and then of course, Valentine's Day! I'm sure some of you may love Valentine's Day, and I'm sure some, for whatever reason . . . not so much! Valentine's Day is a major holiday with our family, however. You see, 28 years ago on Valentine's Day, Marty, my husband, officially became my "boyfriend!" I was a mere 13 years old! Of course, at that age, our "dates" were at church youth rallies and he carried my books for me at school and we sat next to each other at lunch with a bunch of other friends, usually playing Uno! (Once we were sent to the office because we were caught holding hands in lunch!) Time sure does fly! SO, every Valentine's Day, we go all out! I decorate almost as much as I do for Christmas! Every year since our son was just a little thing, we make a special "Valentine Box" and we all fill it with valentines and little gifts to give each other at our "special" breakfast that I make for my guys every Valentine's morning! It's a beautiful, candlelight break-*

fast, complete with either homemade, heart-shaped chocolate chip pancakes or waffles, chocolate-dipped strawberries, even heart-shaped pats of butter and sparkling pink grape juice in fancy glasses—with, you guessed it, heart-shaped ice cubes! All complete with beautiful Valentine tableware and other special "stuff!" You just wouldn't believe it! Although I'm sure some of you reading this are in the "gag mode" right now, it's a very special time of us celebrating our love for each other and God's love for us! It's also a great time of reminiscing of all that we have been through as a couple and a family, ever since that day 28 years ago when my "dream boat" presented me with my first Valentine and I nearly passed out! (I'm happy to report that he still makes me weak in the knees!) ☺ I'm a firm believer in making life "special" whenever there is an opportunity. There is just too much heartache in this life to not make a special memory whenever possible. Children also find security in special traditions, and that's what I hope to pass on to my son. So, don't forget to make life special for those you love, whenever you can. We are never guaranteed tomorrow!

Time it takes to do special things? TONS!
Work involved? Very costly!
Memories? Priceless!

Our hero's journey continues this week;
I told you, Episode 2 is in *California or Bust!*

A long hauler drive, or a quick jet fly,
—Tune in, or just walk, if you must!

You won't want to miss the *Fontana Feast,*
Of fast and furious feuding machines!

The leading man of this episode,
Happens to be Jeff Gordon,

Fastest to qualify;
The plot thickens with each scene!

From the south of Florida,
To southern California,
The *Hollywood Hotel* embarks!

You can count on "those guys,"
To bring us the most weekly action!
High in the sky is where they'll be parked!

Folks are still stunned over last week's display!
Wondering how in the world did Mark Martin lose that race?!

You just never know,
From one week to the next,

Who will be the leading man,
Or whose Victory Lane scene will be cut instead!

Right now, all eyes are on Brian McKnight!
Whose performance of our National Anthem
Was just outta sight!

Instead of a football,
Troy Aikman *threw* the GREEN!

Which sent the guys rollin'
With a full head of steam!

Our leading man started falling,
Right at the start!

He didn't *miss his lines*,
Just let Kasey Kahne share his part!

Jeff's just playing it safe——
He has Johnson's car set up.

Trying something new,
Because yesterday's practice had him fed up!

The first CAUTION of the day
Came just before lap 8!

Riggs and Sorensen conflicted interest,
Out on the back *straight!*

The front nine stayed out,
And didn't bother to go in and pit.

No need for adjustments yet,
Or even a small petrol sip!

However, there's a fuel-cell change:
From a 22 to an 18-gallon cell!

They'll get 38-42 laps on one tank,
——As far as their "guesstimations" can tell!

Truex blew his engine on lap number 14!
Jeff went in for adjustments and hopes now his car's freed!

18 laps in and Jr.'s right front tire blew!
But the CAUTION shortly after, wasn't caused by this issue.

The restart showed The 24, embroiled in 33rd!
And with 220 to go, The 5 and 17 clamor for first!

When 204-to-go rolls around,
Kenseth's 3.1 seconds out front!

I know it doesn't look like it now,
But Jeff's in 21st and is focused on the hunt!

By lap 49, GREEN pit stops began,
But 4 laps later when the CAUTION came out,
The guys that pit lost the upper hand!

They're now a lap down,
Which is never very fun!

It would have been fine,
Had Sterling Marlin not spun!

189 to go and Jeff's car is decent in seventh place!
Right in front of him is his teammate in Car 48!

But at this "show on the road,"
31 cars are NOT on the lead lap!

Dale Jr.'s day looks done——
——He's in for an engine mishap!

Besides their red cars,
Kasey and Jr. have a lot in common!

Now Kasey's in the garage,
Looks like **his** engine now has problems!

Lap 85 shows our Star is up to sixth!
We knew his back-in-the-pack position
Was something he could fix!

Nothing like a suspense-filled thriller,
To keep you coming back for more!

So have yourself some popcorn,
This feature film is certainly no bore!

The 17 of Kenseth,
Is the leader on 101,

Next it's Stewart, then Jimmie then Bowyer,
And The 24 rounds the top-five *guns!*

Guess who's 45 laps down,
And heading back out on the track?

Jr.'s going to make an attempt,
To get a few of those laps he lost back?

Jeff's out second after a CAUTION for debris!
He dogs the bumper of Matt Kenseth
On this speedway shaped like a "D!"

The 8-car discovered that little "science project,"
That was performed on his car didn't work!

He spun real nice and proudly took a bow
For avoiding the wall——
——You know that would have hurt!

His spin and his exit from his smoking machine,
Was an Oscar-winning performance for sure!

Meanwhile Jeff's on a tear,
And going for the lead!

For Gordon-fan anxiety,
First place is the cure!

He gets it! On lap 135!
But was robbed by The 17 shortly after!

The 17 left a donut on the side of his car!
Which *could have* led to a major disaster!

Stewart snuck up and stole the lead from Matt Kenseth,
The 24 is still in second place!

Then Tony was too fast,
Entering the Pits on GREEN stops,
He'll no longer be leading this race!

Juan Pablo Montoya is "in school" today;
He's admittedly the "new kid" in town!

He's trying to hold on,
Stock car races are much longer,
Than the F-1 series, he found!

With 50 laps to go,
Things get a little interesting . . .
The 48 is now in the lead!

The 17 is in second, Jeff is in third,
Falling back! He's too loose and can't speed!

26 laps to go, and Jeff's going backwards and in fifth!
"That's the wrong way!" I keep yelling!

Then CAUTION number 8, hopefully will save the day!
Tighten him up and what will happen, there's no telling!

With 19 to go,
Harvick and Jeff battle hard for third!

And believe it or not, Stewart's fought back to seventh!
He found a way to weave through the "herd!"

9 laps to go and The 29 is closing on Kenseth!
——Remember it's Harvick who just won last week!

He's clawing mighty hard,
Trying to take the Cup win again,
Here at the end of **this** week!

Like ripping a carpet out from under your feet,
This race stopped dead in its tracks!

The RED flag was thrown,
Reutiman completely destroyed his car!
His front tires were shoved clear up under the dash!

He was out cold for a few seconds,
As we nervously looked on,
Just waiting for him to respond and react!

You know if it weren't for NASCAR's safety devices,
It would have been lethal, you can surely count on that!

Thankfully David's fine, and Pit Road opens,
Jeff stayed out but The 5 and 20 pit!

Then just before the restart,
Harvick has a left-front flat!
This is the end of his hopeful 2-for-2 stint!

Four laps to go, and Jeff is in third!
But takes second from Burton,
And then, my stomach contents curd!

It's Johnson on his bumper,
Jeff's fighting for the lead!

But the checkers came too soon!
Kenseth pulled off the ultimate deed!

Yes the 17 wins, with Jeff only .7 of a second behind!
(Hang on, let me go take a look in my ear,
And see if I still have my mind!)

Johnson is third, then The 31 and Mark Martin!
The first two race finishes so far,
Is a fine way for Jeff's season to be startin'!

Kenseth celebrates too hard and fries his transmission!
Pushing that used-up vehicle to Victory Lane was the 17-
team's ultimate mission!

The roulette continues at Vegas next week!
I put my money on The 24-man and machine!

The odds are looking good at this stage in the game!
But will he hit the jackpot,
Or end up really lame?

That's why I'm not a bettin' woman you see,
No way to predict the future, so please don't ask me!

But if I were a bettin' woman,
I'd certainly make the call——

Hands down, I'd choose Gordon,
To leave Las Vegas, winning it all!

CHAPTER 3

UAW-Daimler Chrysler 400
Las Vegas Motor Speedway

March 11, 2007

*This was actually the first Re-Cap I ever wrote. I was extremely sick for the first two races of this season and could barely function due to writhing pain from Shingles, let alone take notes during the race for a Re-Cap. However, when Vegas came around, I decided to give it a shot and see if I could write a lyrical style re-cap, **just for fun**. Well, the rest is history, and so the re-caps began! It was fun because Jeff was so awesome all day! Until, however, the very end.*

But, as they say, "That's Racin'!"

Here we are in Vegas
The stakes are already high . . .

. . . Not the best starting spot for Jeff,
We cannot lie.

But it won't be a problem for the 24-crew,
Mr. Steve and our driver will know just what to do!

We'll hold on to our seats as he plows through the field,
"Picking" off spots 'cuz he's up on the wheel!

We've seen it before,
We'll see it again,

We know where he's headed,
Who cares where he's been!

As we wait here amidst this great "NASCAR Nation,"
As our palms begin to sweat in anticipation,

We hear the loud call,
No more time's wastin',
"It's show time boys, let's go racin'!"

The pressures are down, the switches are up,
Kasey Kahne leads the field, but Jeff's on his way up!

He's plowing through the field like I said he would do,
Then the CAUTION comes out——even before lap two!

The 6 is in the wall, he got out of his groove,
But keep your eye on 24 'cuz he's on the move!

We got rollin' again, then on the 9th lap,
Jeff misses a wreck and a mess on the track!

This melee took out Casey, Ward Burton, and Robby,
But our Jeff gained 3 spots 'cuz he knows how to lobby!

Lap 14 it's Sadler who takes up the lead,
But look out Elliot, our boy found some speed!

The grip was poor on the hot, slick track!
More CAUTIONs came out, but Jeff came from the back!

He stayed out, didn't pit, now he's in 6th;
We Gordon fans are glad he stayed clear of the Pits!

On lap 24 Jeff is in 5th,
Then he moves up to 4th on lap 26!

Jeff's "super loose" on lap 28,
Kyle Busch is flyin' and is in 2nd place!

The 24-fans,
Listening in,
Hear Jeff state—"worst conditions he's ever raced in!"

No time to panic, we don't need to spin!
Hang on to that carriage and go for the win!

Through a series of leaders and adjustments and more,
Jeff's good in 1 & 2, but "wicked loose" in 3 and 4.

"Never Fear," says "Super Steve,"
"we'll lower the track bar again;
Just keep doin' your thing no matter what shape you're in!"

Lap 61 and Jeff is in 10th,
He passed Carl Edwards!
Can you stand the suspense?!

On lap 95, the 24-car's up front!
We're in 4th spot now, and we feel like we've won!

Starting 36th (No, I'm not jokin'!)
Is a thing of the past "Baby," that Nicorette car is smokin'!

The lap 106 CAUTION,
To Johnny Sauter was a curse,

But Jeff's 2-tire stop puts him out FIRST!!

On lap 116, two Hendrick cars are down,
And Jimmie's back in the pack
'Cuz his tire rolled out of bounds!

Meanwhile Jeff's cruisin' with a 3-second lead,
And wonders to himself, "Can we hang on to this speed?!"

This high-stakes race in the city called "Sin"
Had more CAUTIONS and PIT STOPS,
Then Menard took a spin.

74 laps to go, and guess who's behind Jeff?
It's the 48-car,
Yes, Jimmie Johnson, no less!

From Jeff to Jimmie is a 2½ second gap——
We love ya Jimmie,
But we love ya best off Jeff's back!

After the lap 225 CAUTION,
Remain 35 laps and the DuPont Chevy's still AWESOME!

In front of the pack, our Jeff still remains,
Then all of a sudden, he makes us insane!

He thinks he's got a tire that might be going down!
"You've got to be kidding!" "Get out of town!"

The air left my body, I about lost my lunch,
In the nick of time Jeff says, "I think it's just junk!"

Just junk on the tires and not really a flat?
"I'm an old man," says Letarte,
"I can't handle that!"

"Welcome to my world," I say,
As I collect my condition,

We can't give Burton the lead
Due to that kind of attrition!!

Lap 231, and Burton's not our worry,
Jimmie takes the lead, and he looks in a hurry!

Jeff states to Stevie, "This car's not the same"
He's only 2nd to Jimmie, but his car's slightly lame.

Jeff's led the most laps,
Came to the front from the back,
Is a win at Vegas too much to ask?

Our luck needs to change,
Only five laps to go!

We're running behind,
Only 1.3 seconds too slow!

It's a 1,2 finish for HMS.
Jimmie grabbed the "checkers"
And then Jeff was next.

It's the 150th win for the Hendrick organization,
And all HMS teams are filled with elation!

You and I both know
Where most of those wins came from,
And we all win the Jackpot because we root for #1!!

What a great effort by the 24-team!
They gave Jeff a car that was lean, mean and green!!

Great calls all day——you know it's a gamble!
And at the last minute, Chad had the handle!

But the "MOJO" is flowin' for Team 24,
Watch out Atlanta, we're comin' back for more!!

CHAPTER 4

Kobalt Tools 500
Atlanta Motor Speedway

March 18, 2007

This Re-Cap was started on schedule, the day after the race on March 19, 2007. However, I never finished it until October 4, 2007! (Thank goodness I keep notes from the race! My memory wouldn't be that keen if I tried!) Anyway, the delay in the Re-Cap is due to the fact that my dearly beloved husband, Marty, was riding his bike on Saturday, March 17th, and was hit by a car! He was taken to the hospital by ambulance where he received 31 stitches in his forehead above his right eye. He had many other "bang-ups" and bruises, including a fractured wrist and disc issues in his neck and back. SO, as you can imagine, Monday was filled with phone calls with insurance companies, calls to make appointments with the orthopedic doctor, plastic surgeon, and chiropractor, and we had to go back in to have his stitches checked. Needless to say, that entire week was completely crazy! SO, that is why I never had time to finish the Re-Cap until October! But, when all is said and done, I am so very thankful my husband is alive and well!

Praise God! It could have been so much worse!

SHHHH, can you hear it?
The thunder in the air?
It's coming from the deep, Deep South!

Yes, just south of Atlanta
There's a super "quad-oval"
Where a storm's comin', of this there's no doubt!

As you bend your ear toward the Atlanta Motor Speedway,
"March Madness" is here at last!

With dark clouds of smoke, and rubber that's burnin'
We're at the home of real racin', real fast!

Gordon starts the race with some impressive statistics,
Here at this "Peach City" track,

Only time will tell if his finish will be "peachy,"
And he'll add to those great winning stats!

You've got 500 miles to be "on top of your game,"
As you search for your ideal groove.

With 54-degree air temps and a rough, rugged surface,
That flame-car will know how to move!

Lap 1 starts us off with a Hendrick car trio,
First Jimmie, then Jeff and then Kyle.

With Jimmie in the lead and Jeff right behind,
This looks like the end——Vegas style!

"D.W." makes a comment about our "24-guy,"
How he "Always seems to adapt."

That "Even if he doesn't seem to be running that well,
He finds *something* that no one else has!"

On lap 20 the 5 seems to have a vibration.
Lap 22, Jr.'s in the top 10.

On lap 24, Jeff's entry is better,
But on 27, he's real tight, again!

On lap 32, Jeff is barreling through,
Cutting into Jimmie's four-second lead.

Jeff's reelin' him in, Stewart's just behind him,
"CAUTION'S OUT!" Said those three guys on *Speed!*

It's lap 35, and the pits come alive,
"Small wedge adjustment," is what "Stevie" said.

The pit crew was on it, here in "Hotlanta,"
And got Jeff to the lead once again!

On lap 42, Jeff lost the lead to "Tony Stew,"
And on 52, he cries out to Steve:

"Didn't do enough, guys,
We need more next time,
If we want to get back to the lead!"

By lap 76, the drivers discover,
That tire wear is surely an issue!

Lap 80, Jeff's in eighth, Jimmie's leading the race,
And Letarte ponders just what he should do!

By lap 99, Jeff's doin' fine,
Goes by Earnhardt and takes sixth position!

He keeps diggin' and workin' along with his crew,
'Cuz that DuPont car is on a great mission!

Lap 167, Jeff's back to the front,
Where once again he takes the lead!

Over a thousand laps led, more than all active drivers,
Due to HMS power and speed!

Lap 192, Steve needs Jeff to come in.
Oh no! His right front hangs in the fender!

The car's not the same,
It's "pushin' and loose,"
What it needs now is a real good defender!

Lap 222, Rigs' engine just blew,
Bringing out the YELLOW flag once again.

Time now to fix Jeff's machine, "sorry" said Steve.
As the guys worked for a long 57.9 pit!

There's 19 on the lead lap and Jeff's in the back
When lap 230 brings yet another CAUTION!

We've got to take this chance, to better this car,
And try to get rid of the issues that are rotten!

Well, Jeff's a lap down, and hovering in the back,
And fighting for the Lucky Dog position!

So early in the season, and I'm balding already!
From pulling my hair out, not from lack of nutrition!

Lap 281, Jeff goes by Robby Gordon,
And now he's in the "free pass" position! Awesome!

Robby's all over Jeff's bumper, getting him loose,
Jeff holds him off and now we could sure use a caution!

As if I had a genie and a lamp here in my hand,
Just a few laps later and Jeff gains back his lap!

Lap 317, just a short way to go!
He knocks off Labonte and then three more!

Jimmie and Tony are both fighting for the lead!
Which guy will finish number one in speed?!

Jeff's by Jamie for fourteenth; Earnhardt is next!
Jimmie takes the lead and Stewart brushes the fence!

The 24 got by Stremme for one more position!
Twelfth place is the spot where he'll land for the finish.

Jimmie won again, the ninth time at this place!
It was a hard fought battle leaving Stewart in second place.

Kenseth is third, Jeff Burton, then Montoya.
I'm happy for Jimmie, but to the Gordon team, most loyal!

I want Jeff to win every race of the week!
A little unrealistic, but it's the truth that I speak!

You know for Jeff and the team,
Twelfth place just won't cut it!

They'll work overtime this week
To get that car where Jeff can run it!

With the "Refuse to Lose" attitude
and "bulldog blood" in their veins,
They'll snarl into Bristol with one goal for the day!

To debut that new COT car in Victory Lane,
Would be a great start to some COT dominance fame!

So wait if you can, until Bristol next week!
For action and adventure and the win that we'll seek!

CHAPTER 5

Food City 500
Bristol Motor Speedway

March 25, 2007

Today's race was the debut of the new Car of Tomorrow (COT). These things are like Sherman tanks on steroids! NASCAR developed this new car design for increased safety reasons, and to hopefully even out the "playing field." (We'll see about that!) There are many pros and cons with this new car, but obviously the Hendrick teams have figured them out! Jeff finished 3rd, with his teammate, Kyle Busch being first to cross the finish line. So close and yet so far for Jeff! Oh well, we'll get 'em next time! Former legendary drivers were honored this week, and involved in the start to the race, with Junior Johnson as the commanding Grand Marshall, and Darrell Waltrip waving the GREEN flag!

This week it's "Thunder Valley,"
Where the "jet machines" fly low.

Enclosed within a coliseum,
We await the sold-out show!

With the debut of the new NASCAR COT,
We'll see how it stands the Bristol licks!

With Jeff Gordon positioned on the pole,
Leading this pack of "fast flying bricks!"

Like watching "Mystery Theatre,"
We wait for the unknowns.

Today the temps are hot and slick,
Unlike last year's freakish snow!

"D.W." flies the green——
Waves it proudly from the stand!

"Boogity, Boogity, Boogity, Boys!"
Will you last 500 laps?

We notice damage on Yeley's car,
Even before the race got started!

All the work his crew put in that thing,
I'm sure they're broken-hearted!

160,000 fans are standing on their feet!
And on lap 8 our Jeff slips back,
And Stewart takes the lead.

On lap 17 the "YELLOW's" out,
Reed Sorensen takes a spin.

Time to work on the DuPont Impala,
And make it better with hopes to win!

Food City 500

The laps press on in this grueling race,
For our driver in The 24!

It's been a backwards slide since we started this thing,
Keep adjusting, Steve, we need more!

We're up to lap 114 now,
And Gordon's falling like a rock!

The crew keeps working, tweaking and freeing,
And in our driver, we still take stock!

"While the children are playing," "D.W." just said,
"Look who's coming toward the front!"

The car that's almost been lapped a number of times,
And has mostly just been junk!

It's that 4-time Champ and his "Refuse to Lose" crew,
Those guys will never give up!

It's perseverance, drive, and steadfastness like this,
That'll help their driver win **THE CUP!**

Gordon somehow miraculously rebounded,
To the second place position!

It will be a GREEN, WHITE, checker finish!
To be behind no one was his mission!

Jeff's fans are tense and sweating,
No, downright "ulceritic!"

Will it be "checkers or wreckers" in these final laps?
Or will another HMS driver win it?!

The restart finds Kyle, in Car Number 5,
The only obstacle in front of Jeff!

But the 24's tight, so Burton plows by,
And there just aren't enough laps left!

But all is not lost for our "big picture" guy,
As he's now **first in points** where we like him!

His young teammate, Kyle, wins the first COT race.
Chevy's 600th win also owned by him!

More milestones created in this Food City 500,
It's the 3rd straight Hendrick win this year!

And Rick's 200th victory for NASCAR thus far,
UNTIL NEXT WEEK, when our Jeff instills fear!

It's Martinsville, Baby, where Jeff can't be beat!
So, "Hickory, Dickory, Dock . . ."

I predict at this very allotment next week,
Jeff will have earned another Martinsville clock!

He's won there before; he'll win there again,
Oh yes, you just stay tuned!

There are 42 drivers (Jeff Gordon's not one!)
Whose Virginia future looks DOOMED!!

CHAPTER 6

Goody's Cool Orange 500
Martinsville Speedway

April 1, 2007

*W*ith all of the wins and dominance Jeff has had at this place, whenever we come here, we fully expect him to win! (Unless, of course, a 5 lb. hunk of track decides to blow a hole through the front of his car like it did a few years ago!) Today was no exception! AND, we were so hungry for a win we could taste it! Watching team-mate Jimmie Johnson lead at the end with Jeff riding his bumper, it became painfully clear that Jimmie wasn't about to pull over and let Jeff go by, nor was Jeff going to "move" him out of the way like some of us from the "Gordon Fan Camp" would have liked to have seen! (Sorry, Jimmie!) I guess our Victory celebration will have to wait! Does anyone have any idea how much I hate to wait?!

"Patience is a Virtue,"
I know. I'm trying, Lord, but it's not easy!

History shows a lot of things
From prior days gone by . . .

The oldest, shortest NASCAR track,
Its archives just don't lie!

Where else can you hear the freight trains rumble,
Both on and off the track?

And afford the world's greatest "tube steak" around,
Even if it's money that you lack!

"Two bucks" will buy you a "Jesse Jones dog,"
And with it you'll see priceless entertainment!

On this paper clip track with its tight pit stalls,
And a propensity for tempers to wear thin!

There'll be 43 guys in a "bumper to bumper" grind,
Counting down 500 laps!

But if you wonder how it's done,
"Pay attention, son!"
That 24-car's got it down pat!

He's got 7 wins down, he's not clownin' around!
At this place, he really gets "toolin'!"

Just watch him today, another win's on the way!
That's the facts, Jack, I ain't "April Foolin'!"

"Gentlemen, start your engines," was Richard Petty's cry!
Jeff's third on the grid where he'll start.

The switches are flipped, the GREEN flag waves,
And Jeff begins to work his "Martinsville Art!"

He goes after McMurry in only lap 3,
Then Casey Mears goes for a spin!

Back to GREEN on lap 8,
After Casey's "Mear" skate,
That revealed a broken sway bar for him!

On lap 23, Hamlin laps Allmendinger,
And Jeff's car is getting free on the exit.

Not a problem for him, he can drive that machine!
Whether COT car, Ferrari or Lexus!

On lap 55, there's a crossover pass,
As our favorite guy takes over the lead!

Though he's a "little loose off and a little loose in,"
It's obvious our man found some speed!

It's a "bumper tag" game of "follow the leader,"
As lap traffic clogs up the track!

A lap 89 CAUTION sends Jeff in for adjustments,
And he comes out first, not looking back!

In only 10 more laps, another YELLOW is flown,
But in first position The 24 still sits!

They've made some adjustments,
And are working real hard,
And doing an incredible job in the pits!

On lap 107, Jeff's pulling away,
With Hamlin and Harvick on the hunt!

On 137, The 11 takes the lead,
And Gordon fans aren't pleased with this stunt!

More CAUTIONS fly, with the rain clouds nearby,
When **ALL OF A SUDDEN SOMETHING HAPPENS!!**

Jeff's lead is lost, something is wrong!
And at least 10 cars surge quickly by him!

This Martinsville track has been known to "attack",
Could this possibly be happening again?

Or is it a flat, some "marbles" or rubber?
On the lap 246 CAUTION they'll check!

They examine the Chevy with surgical precision,
Checking every lug nut and spec!

It's still a mystery today, what got in Jeff's way,
And sent him back to 15th in the deck!!

Now with the bad weather threatening,
And we've passed halfway now,
Panic courses through all of our veins!

But Jeff's peggin' them off, one at a time,
And goes for the leader in car number 8!

Lap 288, and "Happy Harvick's" not happy!
The cable of his fuel pump has died!

After a lap 305 CAUTION, that "flaming" Impala,
Has moved up, hoping his win's not denied!

Well, there are storms just a brewin' all over the place,
Not just above in that big 'ole grey sky!

On lap 326, three Hendrick cars are "on it,"
With Jimmie, Kyle and Jeff in the top 5!

The "CAUTION's Out,"
On lap 335,
Which is fine with us fans who are watching!

Bunch 'em up again!
Race the rain and each other!
Then lap 353 imparts the 10th CAUTION.

Lap 357, the rain is here,
And NASCAR throws down the RED flag!

Just a short break,
We're dry by 363,
Let's get back to racin' and quit with this lag!

Jeff takes the GREEN,
Behind Bowyer and Jr.
Right now, he lays back in third.

With his blowers aimed straight,
On those hot, warn brakes,
You know what he's going for is first!

The next CAUTION finds Jeff,
Restarting in 10th,
With nine other cars in his way!

He "shuts the door" on some more,
And then shows up in second
For a wicked duel with Car 48!

The two teammates battle,
With way too much kindness,
In what seems like an endless charade!

24-fans scream loudly,
To the point of exhaustion,
For Jeff to "punt" Jimmie out of the way!

One thing for sure,
Team 48 can be thankful,
It was Jeff in the runner-up position!

Our gentleman Champ
Showed mercy and class,
Instead of cheap, selfish attrition!

He's still a legend, as he proved here today,
At this crazy, Martinsville track!

With even more drive to win,
As he heads south to Texas!

He'll be bigger . . .
He'll be "badder". . .
HE'LL BE BACK!!

CHAPTER 7

Samsung 500
Texas Motor Speedway

April 15, 2007

Most of you know, especially if you are a Jeff Gordon fan, that Jeff has yet to win at this Texas track. He has been so close on several occasions! We sure thought all of that was going to change today! He definitely looked like the car to beat! Must we run into walls?! (Easy for me to say!) At least we have a top 5 finish, and at least he's still first in points. (I'm trying to look on the bright side here! Aren't you proud of me?) However, we are still waiting for that first win of the 2007 season! This patience thing is getting old!
"The 'beef' goes on . . . !"

There's a lot of cattle in Texas,
Just a roamin' on the range,

But the biggest "beef" in this Lone Star state,
Is with a speedway and a car with flames!

You see our 24-guy has won everywhere,
Except for Homestead, Phoenix and Texas!

It's time we got down and dirty,
And crossed that last one off our checklist!

He's a Super Star in the Lone Star state,
Fired up for a "Texas Hold 'em!"

Where he starts on the pole
And hopes to end there too,
At this 1½ mile oval!

"Everything's bigger in Texas," they say,
Including our hopes to see a Jeff Gordon dominance!

The 24 wants to see, another HMS win,
And make it a fifth straight Hendrick car prominence!

It's a hot, slick day, after some crazy wind and rain,
And "Stone Cold" calls to "Start Your Engines!"

Up high in the sky, flies the B-52,
And two Jeffs start us off here in Texas!

Gordon holds off Burton,
And collects five points,
For leading the very first lap!

Then the CAUTION flag flies,
And it doesn't look pretty,
There's an on-track shatter and slap!

Turn 4 is the place, at the start of this race,
Where The 6 pushes up into Yeley.

Then all of a sudden, here comes Ricky Rudd,
And joins The 6 in a "piggy back" melee!

We re-start on lap 7,
With our Jeff in the lead,
And from Jimmie, he's driving away!

It's obvious to see,
The 24 means business,
And brought an awesome machine here today!

On lap 24, he's stretching it out,
With a 2½-second lead!

While The 29's falling back,
Says he's extremely tight,
And plummets and loses some speed.

On lap 43, Jeff's in heavy lap traffic,
By now, it's clearly understood,

That of all of the 42 "neighbors" The 24 has,
He's surely the best in "The Hood!"

A lap 43 CAUTION, involving Mike Bliss,
Who got really loose and then wrecked.

Lap 68 and Hamlin feels a vibration,
His rear wheel was not "up to spec"!

On lap 72, Mike Joy makes a statement,
Says, "Gordon's pretty firmly in command!"

After GREEN flag pits, and a slight wedge adjustment,
I'd "bet the farm" today's winner would be our man!

Something cool happened on lap 104,
At exactly 2:**24** pm (Texas time),

I looked at my screen, and right away noticed,
Jeff was 2.**24** seconds ahead!

A trivial fact for some, yet intriguing to others,
I thought I'd throw that in "for FREE!"

But the real truth is,
There's nothing trivial about
A 2.24 second lead!!!!

The wall is in the way, for Newman and Menard,
Then a lap 115 CAUTION for debris.

Which stinks for the fans of the 24-car,
'Cuz it erases Jeff's 4-second lead!!

Only 17 cars on the lead lap now,
And on lap 123 The 8 steals second place.

The 48's not happy, when Jr. cruises by;
Somethin' strange is "brewin' here in this race!

Lap 153, Jr. takes the lead,
As Jeff states, his car's "really bad!"

Lap 169, it's GREEN-flag pit time,
Can the guys give the car back what it had?

Somewhere between lap 190 and 200,
The 41 has trouble with his engine!

Samsung 500

On lap 202, Jeff and Jimmie duke it out,
For position, you see they both wanted second!

Lap 228 is a bummer for The 48,
He seems to have problems with his motor!

Then it's Kyle's turn, on 234,
Wondering if engine trouble will mean his race is over!

The next problem occurred on lap 238,
When Juan Pablo and Stewart got together.

"Smoke" went around and then "T-boned" Jimmie,
What The 48 hoped would not happen ever!

From here on out, Jeff Gordon fans battle,
With heartburn in a major way!

He goes in to pit and loses 6 spots,
Now he's all the way back in eighth!

With 83 to go, Jeff moves up to seventh,
He's inching back up to the front!

On lap 252, Stewart, Jr. and Kyle,
Pull an on-track, non-graceful stunt!

This CAUTION brings Jeff straight to the pits,
For a 2-tire stop, gaining some positions!

Lap 272, Jeff takes third from Mark Martin,
Then takes second on 276!

Just to put the fans, right over the edge,
On lap 290, Jeff slams the wall!

"Pass the antacid, please . . . the whole bottle, please!"
I'm thinking of taking them all!

Jeff finally pits and the crew puts him out FIRST,
With only 38 laps now to go!

The clean air is yours; now put the "peddle to the metal,"
Show Texas who's "King of the Road!"

Jeff's 1 ½ seconds ahead, then hits the wall again!
And Kenseth goes by Jeff right away!

Then on 321, Burton's by Jeff,
Another car in The 24's way!!

Lap 325 proved to be weird,
When The 5-car came out with Jr. as the driver!

Jeff led the most laps ends up in fourth
And remains a top five survivor!

Another win lost, slipped through our fingers,
And the wrong Jeff's in Victory Lane!

The *Psych* Ward is busy, across the country today,
Because all the Gordon fans have gone completely INSANE!

But next week is Phoenix,
In the blazing hot desert,
Where the flame car will be burning for sure!

Tomorrow is "tax day" but today was more taxing!
But next weeks WIN will surely be THE CURE!

CHAPTER 8

Subway Fresh Fit 500
Phoenix International Raceway

April 21, 2007

–Honoring Jeff, and the Victims of Virginia Tech–

Jeff's first win of the season, sadly, was overshadowed by the shocking massacre that happened this week at Virginia Tech. Thirty-three lives were senselessly taken. Today is an incredible example of the highs and lows of life. To all of you who have lost loved ones from the shooting, I want you to know how I grieve with you over your losses! You have truly been in my thoughts and prayers, and will continue to be. Please know that God is your un-wavering refuge and is there for all who reach out to Him. He feels your pain. After all, His only Son was massacred, only willingly, for you and for me.

Jeff, I want you to know how proud your fans are of you! Congratulations on these incredible accomplishments of finally winning at Phoenix, and winning from the pole! And tying Dale Earnhardt, Sr.'s all-time wins!

Today, we honor those who lost their lives at Virginia Tech, and we are also proud to honor you, our driver!

There's an underwhelming vibe across the PIR today,
Shared by countless across this land,
Whose lives are filled with ache.

My heart goes out to grieving parents,
Husbands, wives and friends.

The loss they feel, the pain and grief,
Is hard to comprehend.

Though sorrow fills the air
We can be thankful we are breathing,

Though it seems so trite to race today,
But the fans, they are not leaving.

We honor Virginia Tech here in this "Valley of the Sun,"
We'll make those "Hokies" proud today,
When all is said and done!

I know they'd want us to celebrate
The life that we've been given,

And continue on, in true "Hokie" spirit, like them,
We fans are driven!

So from sorrow to excitement with reluctance in one swoop.
Let's try to switch our gears;
There are some cars out there to dupe!

With clear, sunny skies at this one mile flat,
Though gray clouds are looming near.

It's time to stoke the heat in this hot desert sun,
And give the competition something to fear!

Subway Fresh Fit 500

Did I mention Jeff Gordon's on the pole again?
It's almost getting to be "Ho Hum!"

It's his 59th pole, and he's tied with "D.W."
Today's record-breaking feats have begun. . . !

Right away Jeff's day starts off kind of strange,
His radio communication's kind of "junky!"

A classic Saturday night battle in the old Wild West,
In a COT car that's chunky and funky!

Jeff leads the first lap, five points in his grip,
And he says "Adios" to the field!

Hamlin tries to give him a "run for his money,"
To rob Jeff of first spot is his deal!

Won't happen this time, then on lap 25,
Jeff states he's "too loose on the exit."

Then on lap 27 there's a duel with The 11,
The next leader's a result of Denny's aggression.

A strange thing occurred, in turn four we just heard,
A trash bag floated right into this space!

This brought the CAUTION on lap 36,
Yes, a "Hefty" brought a halt to this race!

Back to GREEN on 41, but this is short-lived,
It's a YELLOW again on lap 42!

The 6 became sandwiched, between The 48 and 20,
And this "Rookie" didn't know what he should do!

53

Bad luck continues for Jamie McMurray,
Early on it was his air gun that quit!

Now there's plastic on the grill, and his racecar is smoking,
That's not good, so he's off to the pits!

The race marches on and our Jeff keeps on fighting,
But will fluctuate between second and fourth.

The crew keeps on working on this new COT contraption,
The "Drive for 5" keeps them going, of course!

The lap 97 CAUTION just happens to catch
An illegal pit road speeder!

It's the 11-car! And that's good news for us!
He'll be positioned far away from the leader!

Harvick leads for a time, then Stewart takes over,
And it looks like it's his race to win.

Jeff holds on to third behind Tony and Kevin,
But isn't happy with the position he's in!

On 164, Jeff seized second from Harvick,
And right behind him is Car 48!

Jeff fights a tire rub and a whole lot of tension,
And is there now something wrong with his brakes?!

On 275, he's a mile and hour faster,
Than The 20, who's leading this event!

On 279, The 24 has to pit,
A GREEN-stop, 'cuz his tires are spent!

As he journeys down pit road,
The CAUTION is thrown!!

Oh No! Will he be a lap down?
Letarte makes the call, and says he's O.K.

"Check it out, boys, there's a new "Sheriff" in town!"

There's 20 laps left when we go back to GREEN,
With lap cars in front of Jeff's face!

Must there always be a battle, to get to the finish?
I guess that's why they call it a race!

There's a "Wild West" fight, like never seen in the movies,
And a cavalry under Jeff and Tony's hoods!

On 299, Tony swiped the lead from Jeff,
Then something became **clearly understood**:

We know Jeff was thinkin' "There's no way I'm letting,
Another win get by me today!"

He beats his way back by Stewart and says "Sayonara."
"I've got an appointment over in Victory Lane!!!"

With Tony on his tail,
The fans hold their breath,
We can hardly stand the suspense!

Will Jeff get his first win, out here in Phoenix,
Or will he and Stewart end up in the fence?!

Our minds were eased slightly, on lap 302,
The 24-car is pulling away!

He's got a one-second lead,
And puts the distance on Stewart,
And does some **_INCREDIBLE THINGS_** here today!!

He wins from the pole, and that's never been done,
Out here at this Arizona track!

Scratch Phoenix off Jeff's list, of places for no wins,
He shook that "monkey" right off of his back!

He made an HMS sweep, for all current COT car venues,
He seems to know how to drive the "unknown!"

Though not a "cake walk"win for the 24-team,
They are reaping what their hard work has sown!

Speaking of records and various feats,
Accomplished on this very day,

The biggest by far, was tying Dale Sr.'s wins,
It's **76**——and that "3" flag was proudly waved!

"We always knew Jeff Gordon
Would re-write the record books."
Was something that "D.W." stated.

A comment like that makes a 24-fan proud!
Of our "Dominator" we all are elated!

Jeff's wife and un-born daughter are in Victory Lane,
As Jeff lovingly kisses Ingrid's pregnant belly!

The celebration continues,
Under a shower of Pepsi,
What more can he do? **There's no tellin'**!

"Who's your daddy, baby?"
Oh are you in for a surprise!
I hope you will learn early on——

How much you are loved,
Even long before,
You were a "twinkle" in your mom and dad's eyes!

To the fans and friends who are reading this stuff,
We carry bliss from this win through the week!

As we anticipate a great Talladega race,
Don't forget those whose emotions are weak.

Say a prayer for those victims of such senseless crime,
No one thought it would happen at VT.

Hug your kids extra tightly, and all your family and friends,
Count your blessings,
For **life's precious**, you see.

CHAPTER 9

Aaron's 499
Talladega Superspeedway

April 29, 2007

*W*OW! *What a day this turned out to be! Jeff was on the pole, he exceeded the late Dale Earnhardt, Sr.'s all-time win record, and he did it on what would have been Dale's birthday! Cool stuff like that seems to always happen in NASCAR! But along with the excitement of Jeff's second win in a row, several unruly fans in the stands rudely threw bottles and cans at Jeff after the race! The spotters were even concerned for their own safety! Those folks were hauled off by the authorities to be "taught some manners!" Of course, those doing the throwing really wanted Dale, Jr. to win! Well, when all is said and done, I know that both "Dales" are much prouder of Jeff than of their own fans! Oh well, if there is anything to be admired, it's the passion of a NASCAR fan! However, some may need anger management classes!*

All I have to say is, "It's a good day to be a Jeff Gordon fan!"

There's news across the south,
Across the north and east and west,

About a certain fellow,
Breaking records right and left!

I'll give a clue to those of you
Who reside beneath a rock,

How could it be you haven't heard?
Could it be you've really not?!

It's all the talk you hear these days,
The conversation on the street!

About a four-wheeled DuPont Chevy,
That rivals rocket speed!

The man behind the wheel
Is the envy of the rest!

Friends and fans and foes alike,
Know Jeff Gordon is the best!

Just in case you missed the show
On April 29th,

The chess match that lasted 500 miles,
Derived Victory this Talladega night!

The first to roll off and lead the band
Of nervous Cup car drivers,

Was nonetheless than The 24 *again!*
Guiding the hopeful, "Big One" survivors!

And on lap 2, who's that in the lead?
It looks like Sterling Marlin!

Aaron's 499

Lap 4 is a show of 5-wide cars,
Like hungry sharks, they're starvin'!

Jeff figures the way to stay out of trouble
Is to stay out in the front of the pack!

Unlike his teammate in the Car Quest 5,
Who's in fortieth, back in the stack.

Menard and Carl Edwards have some engine issues,
And are out of the race early on.

Then it's Robby Gordon's turn,
Before Dale Jarrett learned,
Of his ignition trouble on lap 41.

It's a GREEN-flag pit on lap 44,
The 24-crew has lightning-fast speed!

Our Jeff is out first!
But for Stewart, it's the worst,

The pit road limit
He surely did exceed!

He's BLACK FLAGGED and put back,
And on lap 55,
Stewart's two seconds from a forty-two car attack!

Then on lap 72,
Could it be, is it true?
A DEBRIS CAUTION puts Tony back on the lead lap?

I thought The 20 was against DEBRIS CAUTIONS,
Could it be now he's eating his words?

A slice of "humble pie" for him and his friend,
"Jacque Debris,"
Break's over, as he tries to resurge!

There's a lap 80 CAUTION,
And Gordon comes out thirteenth——
This number's not unlucky for long!

Though The 8 takes the lead,
And those Jr. fans freak,
It's those Hendrick engines hummin' a song!

The fastest lane seems to be,
Wherever Jeff and Jimmie speed,
The tune of that gets me singin' today!

Stremme briefly leads, on 117,
But falls victim to a "Hendrick Hustle" fray!

Jeff regains the lead,
While Stremme "dances with the stars,"
Surrounded by some true Hendrick muscle!

On lap 124, Casey Mears tries to pit,
And he and Jimmie start a 200-mile-an-hour tussle!

Another YELLOW's put down,
On lap 130,
With a "collidescope" of cars collidin' in it!

Only 52 laps to go,
When we return to GREEN!
Can Jeff come back from twentieth to win it?

"I can't watch," I tell my husband.
"Let me know when he's back up front!"
"I am truly a "vomitous mass!!"

Then Jeff dices away,
Midst a swarm of "angry bees,"
Instead of moving forward, he's falling to the back!!

Another CAUTION flies on lap 161,
Only 23 more to go 'til the "Checkers!!"

CAUTION flag again, on 175,
And for Newman's car, they had to call the "wrecker!"

With Hamlin in the lead,
And only 10 laps to go,
Jeff's back in the fourteenth position!!

We hear him call to "Stevie,"
To pay close attention,
"Everything's about to change right here" in this mission!!

Throwing "CAUTIONS" to the wind,
Those DuPont flames start combusting!
Jeff's incinerating cars one by one!

Like a tank through the desert,
Avoiding the land mines,
You can "smell another victory" will be won!

Then just when you can't hold your breath any longer,
There's a CAUTION on 184!

Reutiman's engine gives up,
And brings a "GREEN/WHITE/CHECKER,"
My contact lenses about exploded to the floor!

Jeff took the lead, in the nick of time,
With 2 fuel-burnin' laps left to run!

What an AWESOME display,
Of "Speed, Guts and Glory,"

It was Jeff's race to win,
AND HE WON!!!

Bottles and cans flew
Looks like a riot's been started!
Those rude fans were cuffed and hauled away!

They can't take the fact that
Their rival "took the cake,"
On the birthday of their hero here today!

Not only that, Jeff EXCEEDED
Their late favorite driver's wins,
With his 77th victory here at this place!!

All you've got to do,
Is check the record books, my friend,
The 24's not a "joker" he's an ACE!

I can't take these races!
They're bad for my heart!
The palpitations are out of control!

My blood pressure soars,
And my nerves are now shot,
Years are docked from the life of this soul!

A fan can't live with NASCAR,
And would be dead without it!
It's a struggle that goes on from within!

So I'll see ya next week,
We'll be back for more!
To cheer Jeff on to a **GREAT RICHMOND WIN!!**

CHAPTER 10

Crown Royal Presents the
Jim Stewart 400
Richmond International Raceway

May 6, 2007

If you ask Jeff Gordon, he will tell you that this is one of his favorite tracks to race at! You'd never know it by the past several finishes here at Richmond! However, with the excitement and momentum from the wins at Phoenix and Talladega the past two weeks, surely his "luck" would change! As ready as we all were to go racing on Saturday night, the weather had other plans! The race was postponed until the next day! Thankfully, the weather and waiting yet one more day for the race was the only true "bummer" of the weekend! Jeff was strong all night and had a great finish at Richmond International Speedway! And it was high time!
Yes! Way to go, Jeff!

We were psyched and ready,
Our man was on the pole!

The "mojo" flowed like the great James River,
From recent wins that rocked our soul!

The crew was poised for promise,
To end the Richmond streak,

Of lousy Richmond finishes,
Today will be unique!

The COT was tuned for triumph!
DuPont colors transcend the field!

A Saturday night at this ¾ mile,
To storm clouds we must yield!

The *rains came down and the floods came up,*
Teams packed up all their gear!

To have to wait until tomorrow to race,
To us fans seems like a year!

So the *Car of Tomorrow* truly is!
Time to work on the virtue of *Patience!*

But at one o' clock come Sunday, boys,
We'll be headlong off to the races!

So the day arrives and we start on time,
No rain clouds looming near!

Just sunny skies, until lap 4,
When a "storm" finds Casey Mears!

"Lighting" struck him from Sauter's car,
And brought out the early YELLOW!

The 25 was really bummed!!
And not a happy fellow!

Lap 20 finds Kahne and Hamlin,
In a "dog fight" for sixth place!

Oh by the way, as you might have assumed,
Jeff's led all the laps in this race!

Until lap 32 when Jimmie stole the lead,
And Jeff was "sideways on entry," he said.

And "no drive off the corner," he shared with Letarte!
(It can't be too bad with the laps that he's led!)

The COMP. YELLOW on lap 40,
Allows the crew to work hard on the Chevy,
Which helped Jeff to cruise his way out first!

(I think now's a good time,
To throw down a Pepsi,
And combat this feeling of thirst!)

There's a three-car breakaway on lap 77,
It's The 24, The 8 and then Johnson.

Lap 90 reports that Jeff leads "Jr." by a second!
It's obvious his strength remains constant!

The "Field of Dreamers," on lap 95,
Is a nightmare for those at the end!

As Jeff's picking them off, one at a time!
To get lapped is a bad dream for them!

The CAUTION flag's out on lap 103,
As Sadler's right front displayed a "blow out!"

The 24-team's still "on it" and makes minor adjustments,
Jeff's first and he's stout, there's just no doubt!

With style and grace, in the middle of this race,
Montoya and Sauter "dance" to the wall!

With help from The 12, whom The 42 blames,
And he swears that it wasn't his fault!

Sauter's dance partner changed,
At the end of his stop,
A new silent partner hooked up to his rear . . .

. . . It's a "Saws All" stuck there,
And it doesn't belong!
Of a penalty he has reason to fear!

On lap 125, there's a real wicked fight,
Between The 24, The 11 and Harvick!

They all want first place, this time Denny wins out,
First spot now belongs to this maverick!

Harvick and Hamlin "duke it out" for first,
While Jeff observes from back in third place!

The 31 has woes, as his engine decides to blow,
And Jeff Burton is forced off of the pace!

On lap 224, Jeff's positioned in fourth,
He tells Steve the car *stinks* through the middle!

On lap 251, the CAUTION is thrown,
And the track bar's wound down just a little!

There's confusion in the pits,
For Harvick and The 6,
Who crashed when they were blind to each other!

Ragan pits backwards,
And Harvick's too fast!
Some stops just aren't worth the bother!

On lap 269, there's three Hendrick's in line,
In second, third and fourth race positions.

Kurt Bush leads the train,
But it won't stay this way,
After CAUTION Jimmie leads the Hendrick exposition!

On 285, the YELLOW's alive,
When The 66 puts Earnhardt in a spin!

Lap 300 finds our Jeff up to second!
"But come on please," "Get the lead out of your spoiler
and win!"

From lap 317 to lap 371,
You won't believe, but **six CAUTIONS** are thrown!

Could hair grow on this track,
And bring out the next YELLOW,
Incited by this testosterone show?!

Whether Car of Tomorrow, yesterday or today,
Those Hendrick cars dominate the rest!

Yeah, The 48 wins, then Kyle then Hamlin,
But we know the guy in fourth place is **THE BEST!**

He led the most laps in that DuPont Impala,
The Richmond rivalry seems to be done!

With eight top fives thus far, and nine top tens,
And two of these races he's won!

Like a tough gladiator in the midst of a coliseum,
Each week there's an awesome display!

Of power and strength and determination,
And teamwork exerted all day!

"The Lady in Black" waits in anticipation!
We'll see if she's "too tough to tame!"

With thermodynamics and shear fearless valor,
"The Lady," The 24 will enslave!

CHAPTER 11

Dodge Avenger 500
Darlington Raceway

May 13, 2007

*T*oday is Mother's Day! I would first like to start out by wishing all of the moms out there a very happy one! Mother's Day is one of my favorite holidays! Not solely because I usually get some sort of a much-needed break that day (!), or because of the showering of gifts and attention, but it causes me to reflect on the blessing of being a mom! I usually think back to the day I gave birth to my son, and nearly lost my life in the process! Anthony was 5½ weeks early due to my severe toxemia! It was NOT the happy birth that a lot of couples enjoy, with a candlelight dinner at the hospital, and many visits from well-wishers! Instead it was filled with pain and suffering and fighting for my life! However, as miracles would have it, Anthony was fine and at a good weight and development (6 lbs., 10 oz.!), even though he was so early! He is now going on 17 years old and 6' 3" tall and a real "hunk" of a guy! (Just like his dad!) You certainly would never guess he was premature! I also think of my own precious mom and the many sacrifices she made for me. (And still makes!) How she ever raised four of us "terrors" is beyond me! She instilled in me so much! Not only did she and my dad teach us *great morals, spiritual wisdom, and values, as well as setting an impeccable example of loving each other and raising a family, but she also instilled in me the love I have for NASCAR! My mom is a GINORMOUS Jeff Gordon fan! We always call each other after the races and express our elation or frustration! I don't think there has ever been a race on Mother's Day before, but because of yesterday's rain delay, some of our special plans were rearranged! We went to the early service at church instead of the later one that we normally attend, went out to dinner and never had to wait in line because we were almost the first customers of the day, AND home in time for an absolutely fantastic race where my driver won under seemingly impossible circumstances! WOW! This was truly the best Mother's Day to date! And, this is just a hunch, but I'll just bet that Jeff's mom is slightly proud of her son! But you don't have to have a child that is a world famous racecar driver to be a proud mom! Anthony, I am SO PROUD to have you for my son! I love you more than words can say! And Mom, you are the World's Greatest Mom, and I am SO thankful for you! Thank you to all of you moms out there who do so much for so little!*

And, thank you, Jeff for winning <u>just for us</u>!
That was way cool of you!

A newborn baby girl was birthed,
50 years in the great beyond,

With back-breaking, relentless labor,
Adjacent to a minnow pond.

Beneath the southern, Carolina sun,
Her "daddy" had plans for this dame!

But he never guessed his "Lady in Black,"
Would become a legend, "Too Tough to Tame!"

Dodge Avenger 500

This "lady" quite quickly earned a worthy reputation,
For her feisty disposition!

She can take on 43 men at a time,
And welcomes the competition!

This "lady's" not your average "Southern Belle,"
Though she can surely be sweet and sassy!

Still she chews up tires and spits the debris,
For a scene that's not real classy!

Gracefully she's aged, for decades thus far,
And has retained her cantankerous charm!

Only a few,
Have left her presence unscathed,
Most scarred from inevitable harm!

The masses still come to lay witness to,
Her contrary inclinations!

Not even Mother's Day could keep folks away,
From the track or the Fox TV station!

So after a rain delay, second week in a row,
The "Lady in Black" was clean and green!

But it didn't take long for her true colors to show,
She got rugged, ill-mannered and mean!

McMurray was Darlington's first "stripe" of the day,
As Bowyer led the first several laps.

Carl Edwards took his place, and then it was Hamlin,
While Jeff Gordon states he's "REALLY, REALLY BAD!"

In lap 108, Jeff's in a peculiar place,
Smack dab in the middle of the "Busches!"

It's a jungle out there, and his car's such a mess,
To Steve he reports that he's speechless!

But Steve "keeps his head" and goes straight to work,
On the YELLOW, which Sorensen brought out.

Yes, lap 116 finds the 24-troops,
Spring to action to try and make that car sound!

Cars are slippin' and slidin' for most of the day,
With many getting "striped" in the process!

While The 24 battles a seemingly hopeless car,
Hanging in the top ten with small progress!

With all the body slamming, appendage crushes all day,
The "black venom" replaced the white walls!

But on lap 238, true evil took over——
"MY TEMPS ARE RISING!!" to "Stevie", Jeff calls!

Lap 246, the temps are still hot,
But Jeff "fires" past Newman for third!

McMurray reports that his left arm is napping!
Any kind of sleeping right now is absurd!

Schrader pounds the wall for a 254 CAUTION,
So Jeff pits to remove some more tape.

Dodge Avenger 500

Later on he gets passed by Hamlin, then Jimmie——
Time to whip out that ole' Super Man cape!

On 284, The 8 moves to eighth,
Then on 300 our hopes start to fall!

Until LeTarte's words,
Rang out loud and clear:

"The 48's leading now, buddy . . .
. . . Time NOW to go get them all!"

By lap 339, The 48 and then Jeff,
Were massively pulling away!

Is second place even possible,
For this over-heated car?

Is Jeff chosen for "The Lady's" next prey?

Well, things are heating up now,
In more ways than one!

Jeff's closing in on Car 48!

He won't be showed up by his teammate and buddy,
With "The Lady" he's wooed for a date!

Well, on 343, it gets real excitin'
As Jimmie dumps the lead for new tires!

What should have happened, didn't,
Jeff didn't go in!
He knows "The Lady" likes her dates worn and tired!

"Desperate times take desperate measures,"
I've heard it said before!

Then just as Gordon pulls away from the field,
Stremme blew, for a CAUTION once more!

Well the DuPont Impala wasn't happy going slow,
It was obvious she was steaming mad!

My Mother's Day dinner was churning within,
And I was going gray so fast, it was sad!

Well, we went back to GREEN with lucky 13 to go,
With some cars blocking Jimmie from Jeff!

With lots of clean air and a 2-second lead,
Can this southern fried engine beat out the rest?

5 laps to go, and The 11 reels him closer,
Then Jeff yells to Steve, **"THERE'S NO WAY!"**

"Keep diggin', and prayin' and ignore your rear mirror,
The best view's out your windshield today!"

Counting down laps was murder for fans,
That well-weathered Chevy WASN'T fine!

Then all of a sudden, "Big Daddy" was FIRST!!!
That "Stanley Steamer" smoked the checkers in time!

With burned out tires and a burned up engine,
"Old Faithful" wins! (In more ways than one!)

With a geyser of steam, and the stench of the engine,
The smell of Victory's sweet for our Mother's Day son!

78

Dodge Avenger 500

Letarte and the crew kept their cool under pressure.
Along with that tough Hendrick engine!

And kudos to the driver who hung on to that thing!
To him we most honorably mention!

With his seventh win at this place, and 78 victories to date,
We're a witness to a true NASCAR legend!

He's an example to follow, in skill and technique,
So take notes all you budding, young freshmen!

It's amazing that a race that started rainy and chilly,
Could end up so smokin' hot!

As the momentum powers on,
Our "All Star's" on the money!
Can't wait to see what our Super Star's got!!!!

CHAPTER 12

Coca-Cola 600
Lowe's Motor Speedway

May 27, 2007

After a fun weekend last week for the All-Star races at Lowe's Motor Speedway, today we are back to points-racing business as usual! All the "hoopla" is over, and Kevin Harvick walked away with the million-dollar prize! My friend Robyn should be ecstatic, as Kevin is her driver! Congrats, Robyn! Now, here we are, the longest race of the season! Six hundred miles of terror on Memorial Day weekend! With all the holiday and racing festivities, don't forget to pause and remember those who gave their lives for the countless freedoms we all enjoy and take for granted every day! Now that's terror! Don't forget to pray for those who are still fighting so we can remain free! Even on our worst day, we can always be thankful for something, and if you really started writing down what you are grateful for . . . well, you could write your own book! Go ahead, just start jotting some things down . . . Here, I'll help you get started:
How about that air you're breathing?!

We had a week of dramatic sport,
And racing just for fun,

No points to count, just "Shining Stars"
Tryin' to win what Harvick won!

This week it's "back to business,"
Although "usual" it's not!

A 5-hour test of patience and nerve,
And engines running hot!

But look around, this Memorial Day eve,
You can smell the pride in the air!

To the Red, White and Blue,
Which waves high above,
We give a thankful stare!

With race cars decked in military "duds,"
We honor those that serve!

The bagpipers echo "Amazing Grace,"
To remind us of "The Freedom" we just don't deserve!

So as the bugle echoes "Taps"
'Cross the Carolina sky,
And LeAnne belts the Anthem,

Are you truly proud to be an American today,
Or are your freedoms taken for granted?

"From Detroit down to Houston,
And New York to L.A.,"

From every track in NASCAR,
Don't forget to stand and say,

Coca-Cola 600

That you're "Proud to be an American,"
Where at least you know you're FREE!

Where we can watch the Coke 600,
From sea to shining sea!

We can cheer Jeff on from our computers,
At home in our easy chair!

We can watch the action on our color T.V.,
Or if lucky enough, be right there!

So whether by radio, "plasma" or Dell,
Or if you've got a "golden ticket,"

Though Jeff starts back in 32nd,
Watch him machete his way through the thicket!

With a Penske front row——
"The Rocket" and "Duce",
It's not where you start that means the most!

But who ends up front
And wins the long-fought battle,
To this guy we will "toast!"

Only 9 laps in,
And those cool blue flames,
Have burned up to 21st!

Yeah, we qualified poorly,
But it's obvious now,
The 24-car's not the worst!

By lap 14, Jeff's faster than the leaders,
Storming the "ramparts" in his way!

On lap 30 there's an invasion of Casey's ninth position,
No friend or foe will be blocking Jeff today!

Kurt Busch is still the leader,
On lap 39;
The 24 "tank" fires by Yeley for eighth!

Soon after there's a CAUTION on lap 46,
A tire blow for Biffle, and The 13's without brakes!

Just as The 24 soldiers by Kyle and Jimmie,
A huge fracas breaks out just behind him!

Jimmie loses his tread, and there's a multi-car melee!
"Jimmie's House" needs cleaning
From the mess that it's now in!

Well the mess is cleaned up,
And Jeff's up to fifth,
And those top four boys are now sweatin' bullets!

Headed for the front line,
To "take care of business,"
Then there came a sharp pain in my gullet!

You see, all of a sudden,
On lap 61,
Out of the clear blue sky,

The "surprise attack" occurred,
And Tony Raines' "destroyer"
Sent Jeff's "cruiser" its devastating blithe!

Coca-Cola 600

Headlong he sent Jeff,
Straight into the fence,
Then Allmendinger launched him like a missile!

Is that wad of light blue metal,
That just moments before,
Was defensive and clean as a whistle?

Well that "Department of Defense Chevy,"
And our God up above,
Protected Jeff from cataclysmic lethal harm!

Only 28 cars remain,
On the lead lap, you see,
Jeff's not the only car that this early "bought the farm!"

As Jeff goes home to Ingrid,
Where she sees that he's O.K.,
Perhaps some Fritos and a Pepsi's on his menu!

Sure he wanted to watch the race,
But I have a sneaking suspicion,
That from his couch was not first choice for this venue!

So our attention now turns,
To the remaining "Hendrick Herd,"
Only a *few hundred* more miles to the finish!

As I groan in my chair,
Lament that Jeff is not there,
And try and write something exciting so you'll read this!

We're 100 laps in,
Kyle Busch is in fifth,
Next is Jimmie in ninth and Casey in twelfth.

The Hendrick chemistry has been awesome!
Check race history and you'll find,
The HMS boys have the competition squelched!

A lap 139 YELLOW, for debris on the track,
Finds Mears speeding too fast on his exit!

To the back of the pack he's sent,
To work his way back up again,

Can he do it?
Oh yeah, baby, you betcha!

There's a clamor for first, on lap 148,
Between two "Young Guns,"
——Looks like Kyle and Vickers!

Before you know it, it's Jimmie,
And Brian going at it,
Who both could use a new pair of "stickers!"

Well Jimmie takes the lead on 184,
A little later, Brian has power steering issues!

A new "war" breaks out,
Between The 5 and his car,

After one problem turned up,
Another one ensues!

As frustration bleeds,
Through the entire 5-team,
And 147 laps left to endure!

The crew pours over the mess,
That this 5-car is in,
Doesn't look like a victory for Kyle today, for sure!

Kasey Kahne "pancakes" his right side,
For a lap 266 CAUTION.
The 48 came out first for the lead!

He and Kenseth and Stewart,
Breakaway from the pack,
The 8 trails close, but could use some more speed!

Later on in the day, The 25 and The 8,
Both covered in "camo," collide!

Could it be that their scheme,
Made them blind to each other,
As the day transitioned into the night?

The 25's up to third behind Stewart and Jimmie,
In hot pursuit of his very first win!

The top 14 "commandos" pit for some "ammo,"
On a CAUTION on lap 336!

Jimmie had some trouble and he came out in tenth,
It took some time for his "unit" to get him fixed!

This was costly, you see,
Though "His House" may it be,

There'll be a new "renter,"
As his win has been nixed!

Tony's out first,
Charging fast and furious,
In his temporarily-owned "Motherland!"

Casey's 1.8 seconds behind,
And isn't liking the thought,
Of his title being "Second in Command!"

Lap 391 sends Jimmie to the pits,
To re-fuel so he can finish the battle!

Then it's Stewart's turn for gas,
And Jr. takes a brief lead,
When his car starts to "shake, roll and rattle!"

Only six laps to go, and Mears has the lead!
Is there enough precious fluid in his tank?

With the face of an eagle and a finish on fumes,
He'll celebrate his first win dancing to the bank!

High-fives to Darien and the National Guard team,
You've done your country and your teammates so proud!

Another Hendrick *assassin*,
With its weekly valor and strength,
The "homeland security" for these teams remains sound!

You better watch out, and prepare yourself now,
For next week's intrinsic "Shock and Awe!"

That Dover "Concrete Monster"
Doesn't stand a chance,
Against Jeff's 24-gun, long arm of the law!!

CHAPTER 13

Autism Speaks 400
Presented by Visa
Dover International Speedway

June 4, 2007

*T*oday's race is in Dover Delaware, the home of Jeff's title sponsor, DuPont! Of course today's race was supposed to be yesterday, but a little tropical "intruder" by the name of Barry interfered with our plans! Yet another rain delay of 2007! Jeff struggled all day, but ended up with another top 10! Can you believe this team?! Can you believe our driver?! Amazing . . . ! This re-cap also honors the late Bill France, Jr., who passed away today. This news was announced during the race, where we paused to remember the man who helped give us NASCAR and turned it into one of the greatest sports ever beheld by the human eye, or heard by the human ear! I probably never would have been the NASCAR fan I am today had I not witnessed a race via television! Thanks, Mr. France, for your great vision for this "fantasmical" sport! It's because of you that I am the insanely crazed, intensely passionate NASCAR fan that I am today!

The world may not thank you for that, but I sure do! ☺

In the capital city of Dover,
Amidst the urban sprawl,

Lies a wicked, one-mile "Monster,"
Exciting horror in us all!

Some despise its evil skin,
That concrete brawny embrace!

But of all that abhor that rough, rigid oval,
None more than those that race!

You've got to keep that COT car turning!
No down time on the job!

The challenge getting to your pit stop,
Is worse than fighting "The Mob!"

But Victory Lane was eluded,
By another *driver* today,

It was the driving rains of a storm called "Barry"
That had the final say!

The real storm began, the very next day,
To that "mean street" some will concede!

We started at the GREEN,
Ready to "rock and roll,"
With Ryan Newman in the lead!

Our "Super Hero" that has beat this monster villain,
Four times in the past,

Has the pedal to the metal, and is up to fourth,
With his foot hard on the gas!

This proud DuPont town
And scores of fans,
Watch The 24 make his moves!

When the COMPETITION YELLOW flies on lap 25,
The "Man of Steel" comes in to improve!

But he comes out sixth and is despondent to find,
That the Impala is extremely loose!

He accelerated on, with a wiggle and wobble,
Hanging tough though he's "loose as a goose!"

Despite the conditions, the battle persists,
With the "Monster," The COT and The 8!

Jeff seeks to go by Jr. on lap 39,
But for now he'll just have to wait!

The COMP. CAUTION is thrown on lap 65,
Relieved to work on that car once more!

Meanwhile trouble commenced,
For Kyle Busch and his friends,
Over his air hose, the 5-car did soar!

Newman's still in the lead,
On lap 83,
And Jeff's car still is not fixed!

The 99 took the lead,
On lap 108,
And Jr.'s flat sent him limping to the pits!

"Cousin Carl's" in the lead, and then Ryan then Truex,
While Jeff holds his own down in ninth.

The struggle continues and The 1 steels the lead——
Lap 123 finds Martin claiming, "It's mine!"

A CAUTION's put down on 135,
As Kyle slams into the wall!

His bad luck boils over and his frustration compounds,
I doubt that he's happy at all!

Well Jeff's track bar's adjusted,
Along with some wedge,

His tire-wear looks good,
And now he's out tenth!

On 143, Yeley's shock mount is busted,
I told you this track could be tense!

Lap 146 shows The 12 is the leader,
Then Truex, then Carl Edwards is next.

Those 3 guys, must have it together,
Their machines seem to be working just fine!

The 24-car is not up to par,
Something is definitely way out of line!

Jeff's 14 seconds from the leader,
On lap 165,
His "iron horse" just won't tighten up!

Although he and the team keep powering on,
With the mind-set to never give up!

By the 200th lap,
Jeff's unlucky in thirteenth,
Now he feels like he's worn out the right front!

Meanwhile Truex pulls away,
From the rest of the field,
And is 4.3 seconds ahead, what a stunt!

We are desperate to pit,
This car try to fix,
Before we find that we've been put a lap down!

By lap 213, there's fourteen cars left,
Trying to hang tough,
And our Jeff's way back in twelfth!

Meanwhile, Stremme is sick
And needs a new driver!
. . . I could "toss some cookies" here myself!

Jimmie Johnson's up to fifth, on 256!
"What's your set up, Chad?"
"Come on, share the wealth!"

Then everything changed,
At the track here today,
The flags were lowered down to half-staff . . .

Mike Joy announced,
The sad news to us all,
That moments ago, Bill France, Jr., had passed . . .

What a man he was! An iron-fisted force!
That drove NASCAR to what it is today!

His brilliant intellect and strength,
With a lot of hard work,
Allowed no obstacle to stand in his way!

He helped carve out Daytona,
With a dozer and grader,
Moving every piece of dirt with great care!

Because of his vision and plans,
He knew would succeed,
We can now watch our NASCAR on the air!

Now as we humbly pause,
To remember this great legend,
His legacy lives on from this day!

For his family and friends
And all the lives that he touched,
Our love and prayers we humbly send your way.

We must carry on! This race is not over!
Racing's what he'd want us to pursue!

There's a win to be had,
And 43 drivers,
Strive to achieve what he lived for them to do!

The lap 270 CAUTION flew in the nick of time!
The 24 almost went a lap down!

There was an evident tiff,
Between Tony and The 2,
And it's obvious they weren't clowning around!

There were some "hot-headed" actions,
That parked Busch and his car;
To the "Oval Office" he and Tony were ordered!

While Jeff makes several stops
To work on that COT,
And "Stevie" tries to get everything sorted!

Well, a few more YELLOWs,
Due to "Monster beatings."
Things look better on lap 356!

Jeff's seventh on new "stickers,"
He's got 39 laps,
To "Git 'er done" and go for the win!

On 375, Jeff's by Bowyer for sixth,
When with twenty to go, Johnson has a flat!

He's shoved to the back,
As Jeff brushed the wall,
And ends up ninth, which is better than last!!!

What an effort! What a day!!
All are burned out and haggard!
Exhausted and limp from the brawl!

Truex wins his first race,
And Jeff's got a top ten——
Not bad considering the adversity of it all!!

So he and the team
Brush the dirt off their sleeves,
Roll them up and are ready to fight!

To the avalanche of drivers,
In the Pocono Mountains,
The 24-car will be their worst plight!!

CHAPTER 14

Pocono 500
Pocono Raceway

June 10, 2007

Why is it that it always seems to rain at the Pocono's? I wonder if the folks that live there ever get sick of being wet? My husband and I were at this race a few years ago, and, you guessed it, it was a rainy, soupy, sloppy day! (We still had fun, however, but ended up leaving during the rain delay and watching the ending of the race from our beautiful room at Caesar's Pocono Resort! So, it was all good!) But today, TODAY the rain was a blessing in disguise! Jeff and the 24-team saw the rain coming (thanks to Jeff's "eagle-eye" spotter, Shannon!) at almost the official halfway point of the race, and Steve had Jeff stay out instead of going in for a much-needed pit stop! This could have been a lethal decision had we gone back to GREEN, but we didn't, and Jeff and the team celebrated this win with a most appropriate rain dance! Win number four this season, and counting!

Talk about "showers of blessing!" WOO HOO!

The fans and the teams and the drivers are set,
But our fervor is halted 'cause the track is all wet!

This aqueous "stuff" falling hard from the sky,
Causes one to inquire, "Will this 'Long Pond' ever dry?"

It's more like a GINORMOUS, triangular lake!
But the jet dryers forge on 'cuz there's so much at stake!

160,000 fans sitting drenched to the bone,
Wait hour after hour for the great NEXTEL show!

So as those fans in the stands,
Now cold, pruned and wrinkled,

Along with those at home pray:
"**Please**, no more sprinkles!"

The race finally starts,
'Bout the time it should stop,

Late in the day,
About 5 on the dot!

The "Rocket's" on the pole,
With Hamlin as his neighbor,

Can he win four from the pole here?
Is "luck" in his favor?

He needs to watch out,
Another "rocket's" on the track!

Though he's back in eighteenth,
Newman better watch his back!

Here's another "freak of nature,"
To add to the tally thus far—

Pocono 500

Allmendinger over-heats
Before the race even starts!

Denny leads the first lap,
As Jeff quickly advances!

By lap 9 he's in eleventh,
Unafraid to take chances!

GREEN PIT STOPS come on lap 25,
The 24's up to eighth looking valiant and alive!

Lap 48 hosts the first CAUTION of the day,
Robby Gordon blew a tire and there's debris in the way!

Seemed like forever 'til that YELLOW flag flew!
Was NASCAR confused on what they should do?

Jeff's car's really good—
EXCEPT FOR THE BRAKES!

Which can be quite a problem
When you're running a race!

The memories invaded my thoughts about then,
Of that hideous crash that demolished our Jeff!

His brakes became futile at this place just last year,
As he hit the wall hard to our horror and fear!

But racing continues, and on lap 53,
Newman duels Hamlin and takes over the lead.

The YELLOW flew again, by lap 56,
The 22 slammed the wall, helped by the "one six!"

Seven more laps expire——
The *winds of change* were in the air!

Shannon spots some clouds
And reports, "There's rain over there!"

The CAUTION came out, more debris in the way,

Then the most strategic plan supervenes here today!

"Stay out!" "Stevie" said,
Though you need tires and brakes!

I've a feeling this decision
Won't be a mistake!

IF the rains start to come,
You'll be out in first!

But if they don't, this here gamble,
Will be one of the worst!

With clean air in his favor,
Jeff's leading this race!

With The 25 of Casey,
Behind in second place!

To round the top ten,
Third's Ryan then Tony,

Then two "Martins" in a row——(1, 01)
I'm not kidding! No baloney!

Pocono 500

After Mark, there's Nemecheck,
Matt Kenseth then Kyle,

Denny Hamlin's in tenth,
Where he'll stay for a while.

The race is almost half gone
When Jimmie blew a left front!

With sparks and flames flying,
He's out of the hunt!

We're at lap 99, so close to half way!
Some who rarely talk to God were now praying for rain!

No sooner had the fans and the crews said "Amen,"
Was an explosive BOOM of thunder close by from the west!

The "rain dancing" started in the 24-pits!
Apprehension and tension were giving us fits!

The 96-lap-car was blocking Jeff's way!
Jeff's tires are shot, along with his brakes!

The 12 cinches the gap between him and Jeff!
He *almost* gets by him, not a millisecond left!

"CAUTIONS OUT!" 'cuz "IT'S POURING!"
We hear the loud cry!

Part of the track's wet,
While the other part's dry?

The cars are soon parked,
While the dryers blow in vain!

Try and dry this track before dark?
You must be insane!

With 103 laps logged,
Calling this race is **OFFICIAL!**

Though dark clouds loomed above,
"Bad luck" was replaced by a miracle!

What a team! What a crew chief! What a driver that soars!
With drama like this, who'd not come back for more?!

That's ten Hendrick wins of the fourteen thus far!
Four belong to the team of the 24-car!

With fortitude and stamina and a will to survive,
It looks like the "Drive for Five" is ALIVE!

So tune in next week,
Call your friends and your mama!

There's a special on TNT,
Called "A Father's Day Drama!"

It takes place in Michigan,
Starring Jeff and his car!

Supporting roles played
By the best team out there, by far!

There are "good guys" and "bad guys"
and thrilling suspense!
The ending's a mystery, and it's sure to be tense!

Put the roast in the crock-pot and be sure to tune in!
Watch Jeff Gordon contend for '07's fifth win!

CHAPTER 15

Citizens Bank 400
Michigan International Speedway

June 17, 2007

Happy Father's Day to all of you dads out there! I would first like to set the record straight. . . All of you who may think you have the world's greatest dad, well, I'm sorry, you're wrong! Just so you know, I am the proud owner of The World's Greatest Dad! There! Now you don't have to wonder! After all, "everyone is entitled to my opinion," right?! ☺ My dad has been the most incredible example of father and husband I have ever seen! I am truly blessed beyond measure to be his daughter! Thank you, Dad, for your unfailing example of love and commitment. Sadly, a rare thing today. My precious dad is now suffering with a horrible disease called Lewy Body Disease. It breaks my heart more than anyone knows to see him suffer in this way. Even worse that I live so far away from my folks and am not available to help them out more. (I am in south Florida; they are in a tiny "Podunk" town in upstate New York.) Dad still has his sense of humor, though, and that always shines through no matter how he is feeling! I love to call and tell him a joke and hear him struggle to "crack up!" He's so cute . . . And I am so thankful! By the looks of the stands at MIS today, some of you dads received race

tickets for Father's Day! Now that's a huge step up from the usual tie, wouldn't you say?! You were able to see Carl Edwards do his celebratory back flip after his win, but more importantly, see his coach driver and best friend, Tom Giacchi FINALLY be able to cut off that beast of a beard! Since Carl's last win, Tom vowed to not shave again until Carl's next win! Little did he know that it would be 19 months of morphing into "Neanderthal Man!" Who needs a pet ferret when you can grow a "pet" Yeti on your face?! (And the "Yeti" is easy to feed, as it just lives off the leftovers that fall down from your own mouth and gets stuck in its hair!) Eat like a slob and everybody wins! ☺ In any case, I hope you all had a great Father's Day!
And to The World's Greatest Dad, I LOVE YOU!

O.K. you dads, it's your day to "hang loose,"
To relax and enjoy, just whatever you choose!

I hope your Father's Day blessings,
Exceed life's complications,

And you're free to watch the drama
On television's TNT station!

Or maybe you're one of the lucky,
To be in the MIS stands,

Savoring the smell of burnt rubber,
With a cold Pepsi in your hand!

That aroma of fermented petrol,
Simulates frankincense and myrrh to you!

You're a NASCAR DAD, and proud of it, baby!
The priority on today's list of things to do!

Citizens Bank 400

From the "Long Pond" last week,
To the Great Lakes today,
You'd think "fishing" would be first on your brain!

But deep within your soul you know,
A rainbow trout can't compare,

With a "Rainbow Warrior"
Aggressively challenging the fast lane!

Let me open a "can of worms" here,
Feel free to quote, don't paraphrase,

Gordon's the "biggest fish" in any "pond,"
Just let the record books state my case!

Though he's surrounded by "sharks,"
And "steelheads" and more,
Every time he enters a race!

There's also some largemouths" and even a "Marlin"
And "Walleye" Dallenbach covering "The Chase!"

But the "catch of the day" wears familiar flames,
That even a Great Lake can't snuff out!

He's starting in sixth, but is "reeling them in,"
That's what I'm talking about!

It was Yeley's first pole,
But his lead was short-lived,
Jimmie stole it before the first lap!

It's 3-wide racing right away,
On this two-mile D-shape,
Jeff moves quickly to try and tighten the gap!

Jeff told Steve early on,
(Once he plugged his radio back in!)
He could tell "This baby's gonna be slick today!"

His words rang true, and by lap "one two,"
He's up to third accelerating quickly through the fray!

It was GREEN FLAG PITS by lap 36,
Jeff's out third but discovers he's loose!

This is bad for his drivin',
Tryin' to hang on while survivin',
Eighth position is not where our driver would choose!

Lap 65, he's in ninth,
67, he's in tenth,
I begin to expire right along with Jeff's car!

Lap 68's CAUTION saves both of our lives!
This two-tire stop makes him the second-place star!

The 99 was in first, but he was speeding on his exit,
And was called back for some minor chastisement!

Which puts Jeff in the lead, giving him great clean-air speed,
And all his sponsors savor the commanding advertisement!

Lap 74's a BIG WRECK!
Directly behind Jeff!
The lap car of Newman botched this race!

Citizens Bank 400

Thank goodness The 24 was first,
Or he would have been cursed,
With a wadded up car in his face!

Lap 80 shows Jeff and Jimmie first place and second,
Nine laps later, Jimmie swiped away Jeff's lead!

Stewart started forty-first, and is now up to fourth!
It's perceivable his car has highjacked some speed!

Kurt Busch grabbed five bonus points, on lap 109
Trying to make up the 100 lost at Dover!

Jeff "tops off" again, end of 114's CAUTION,
Hoping it'll help him before this furious battle is over!

Edwards is the new leader, by lap 131,
While Jeff's in twenty-first steadily going backwards!

He radios to Steve, the thing that's hindering my speed,
"Feels like I've got three inches of rear stagger!"

Well, with 16 laps to go, Jeff's still in this show,
In eleventh, determined to persevere 'til it's over!

All of a sudden, it's good news for us——
The 48's fuel is done!
Guess today he should have had a lucky clover!

Jeff gains a spot, and "cha ching," some more points!
Then passes "Mikey" for ninth where he'll end.

When all is said and done, he and that 24-team,
Pulled off yet another TOP TEN!!

The winner this day is Carl Edwards! (No way!)
He finally can do his back flip once more!

He's not the only one "flipping out,"
His coach driver and friend,
Can't wait 'til his face is freshly shorn!

As previously promised,
The drama continued,
On TNT today!

It's a tale of "Carl Edwards Scissorhand,"
Who once was a racer,
Turned barber in Victory Lane!

But oh you ain't seen drama,
'Till that "King of the Road Course" cuts loose!

(Unless he's cutting the cord, of his new baby girl
A different kind of Victory will befall frontpage news!)

There should be plenty of "whine" in the Valley next week,
By the 42 drivers he'll beat!

As competition prepares to be violently smoked,
And Sonoma's forecast calls for overwhelming
GORDON HEAT!

CHAPTER 16

Toyota/SaveMart 350
Infineon Raceway

June 24, 2007

I knew when I spoke with Mr. Bickford this week on the 18th, and he said to me, "Maybe something exciting will happen this week and you'll have something good to write about in your next re-cap!" that perhaps, perhaps, this could be **"the week!"** *Well, sure enough, his words delivered! Err, let me get that straight, Ingrid delivered! Beautiful, precious Ella Sofia Gordon was born, and our favorite driver is now a dad! Thank you, Jesus, for the safe delivery! Ella and Ingrid are both doing well, and we are so very grateful! I don't know about you, but I happen to be completely obsessed with baby feet! Whenever any of my friends have babies, the first thing I must kiss are those tiny, wrinkly, adorable miniature replicas of the gross adult versions! Everything about a baby is so precious! From their innocent looks, to their precious tiny lips shaped like the perfect cupid's bow, to their soft breath as it blankets softly on your cheek when you are holding them close! I used to love to watch my son sleep so soundly and listen to his little sighs and squeaks! Please, can you even stand it?! So incredibly precious these "mini humans" are! What a miracle! It's enough to make even the toughest racecar driver feel, well . . .*

Overwhelmed!

OH BABY! WHAT A WEEK FOR OUR FELLA!
IT'S A "VICTORY" ON **WEDENSDAY**
WITH THE BIRTH OF SWEET ELLA!

Of all the great trophies our Champ's held in the past,
This one's soft and pink and more fragile than glass!

Her worth far outweighs diamonds, silver or gold!
A treasure so priceless for her parents to hold!

So much wonder to learn of this gift from Above!
No experience compares with this explosion of love!

But with the scent of fresh baby's breath still in his head,
He kisses "his girls," "Be back soon!"——this he said.

It's off to Sonoma, there's work to be done!
Time to "kick tail" under hot "Cali" sun!

But midst the great joy of the new baby news,
Came some info that plummeted our glee to the blues!

You see, NASCAR discovered a COT car infraction!
The shocking news froze my limbs
Like a head-to-toe traction!

No practice or Qualifying for Jeff and his car?
They have to start from the back,
Where no one's won from that far?!

I was elated, infuriated, hopeful, then ticked!
My emotional roller coaster was on its tenth flip!

But he **HAS** to win this day;
He's done the impossible before!
It's **GOT** to be his race, 'cuz today's the **24th!!**

Ingrid's counting on the winnings to feed Ella Sofia!
My rationale starts to fade, I yell, "What's the idea?!"

I wanted to cry and spit nails all at once!
It's obvious my mental caliber was completely "out to lunch!"

Then from my coffee I took a quick sip,
With my sweaty palm I slapped my face,
And said, "PLEASE, GET A GRIP!"

Though all the punishment's not been dished,
Yes, I'm sure there'll be more!

I can't think of that now,
It's time for some points to be scored!

Jeff's the *king* at this track, lest I slip and forget!
This *might* be his most dynamic win for us yet!

So we suffer through pre-race babble some more,
Wondering what kind of action will befall The 24?!

After what seemed like we waited for most of the day,
Jerry Rice gave the call to get this race underway!

Jeff pulls off (cough) 41st, such a long way to go!
But with strategy and raw power
He'll end at the front of this show!

He knows those twelve turns; he could run 'em in his sleep!
Starting in the rear will just make this contest unique!

McMurray lost his lead rather quickly to Robby Gordon.
Tony's too hot in turn 2 and learns here there's no boredom!

Then The 17, The 45 and 91 do a "dance,"
Which helps Jeff's hot pursuit to quickly advance!

We have a CAUTION on lap 1, where Jeff quickly "tops off!"
It's moves like this that pay off,
And proves why he's "The Boss!"

By lap 12 Jeff's in 26th, one more for four tires and gas!
Then a YELLOW again, Marlin's motor is "dead in the grass!"

Kyle Petty spins on lap 17 for some on-air reporting drama,
I think he's better in the booth——
He and that mic sure have "karma!"

Regardless of this fact, Jeff went by him on 29!
And then by Terry Labonte, now he's 21st in the line!

Montoya and Jimmie push each other around!
Jimmie makes it clear to Juan
He picked the wrong driver to hound!

Jeff's by Truex for nineteenth, by lap 32!
GREEN PITS are next; he's out eleventh, WOO HOO!!!!

By lap 41, Jeff's up to second place!
Do you suppose in this desert
We should start praying for rain?!

Nah, who needs rain when sheer talent abounds!
Jeff pits again when 42 laps roll around.

Now he's behind some "yahoos"
Trying to block his advancing!

They best not "pull on Superman's cape,"
It's not wise to take chances!

Then Steve calls out to Jeff,
A phrase he's been dying to use:

"When those boys are irritating you,
This is how you can't lose"——

"Just picture your new little girl's sweet angelic face,
Relax and drive right by those guys
That are upsetting your race!"

"That's a good one to use," was the proud daddy's reply,
And a couple of laps later, he's by The 12 and 29!

There's a wreck and a CAUTION,
Jarrett's stuck on the track!

Lap 55, Jeff's up to twelfth and he's not looking back!

He knocks off three more and by 61, is up to ninth!
Sorensen pirouettes on 65 and hangs on for dear life!

The 66 and 70 collide on pit road!
Green is on fire for a bona fide show!

At lap 74 things start to shuffle,
As Jeff goes from second to 23rd!

But those in front of Jeff won't be there for long,
They still need to pit, so I heard!

Poor Larry Mac struggles with a "frog" in his throat!
He tries to yell with no voice, and no certain anecdote!

Larry perseveres along with Jeff and the crew!
McMurray's the leader, holding back Montoya's hot pursuit!

With 7 laps to go, Montoya finally takes the lead!
Jeff's up to tenth, but he'll keep going, you'll see!!

He's by Boris Said on 105 for ninth place!
Until Stewart bumps his rear and takes up this space!

Just then Edwards and Jamie's fuel tanks say **"E!"**
Here comes some attrition, and that's fine with me!

Juan Pablo finished first, much to all our "chagrin!"
I was hoping for more empty fuel tanks
To help Jeff take the win!

But his amazing seventh place finish was truly a fete!
Soldiering on to the front, never accepting defeat!

It's Harvick in second, then Burton, then Bowyer,
Biffle, then Stewart, our Jeff and then Kyle.

It's Boris in ninth and Denny rounds the top ten.
J. P. Montoya celebrates his first NEXTEL win!

Though the "grapes of wrath"
Oppressed The 24 and his friends,

Seems the "beatings will continue
Until low morale begins to end!"

But whatever the penalty The 24 will be given,
You can count on the fact that he'll be all the more driven!

The team's vehement attack on Loudon
You know will be cruel!
With an arduous attempt not to break any NASCAR rules!

We'll pray for NASCAR to show some favor and grace!
Stay tuned for an update on this "gray area" case!

Issues like this will be nonessentials in Jeff's life,
When all is brought into perspective
With a look at Ella and his wife!

Intoxicating blessings will replace Sonoma's bitter "whine!"
Next week's win won't hurt, either!

So don't worry fans,
All will commence here just fine!

Two days after Ella was born, I was struck with the desire to write a little song in her honor as a gift to Jeff and Ingrid. I am also a song-writer and a singer, so why not? I heard Jeff say more than once how overwhelmed he and Ingrid were with their new daughter. Hence, the name of the song! The CD single of this song is available, and, like this book, part of the proceeds will go to the Jeff Gordon Foundation as well. Thank you, again, for your support!

Overwhelmed

~ Ella's song

Words and Music by Maria Bennett
Copyright 2007
BMI

Verse 1

Gold and silver, diamonds, pearls
None compare with my little girl
Of all earth's treasures I have known
The greatest in my arms I hold
I'm overwhelmed . . .
I'm overwhelmed . . .

Verse 2

We already loved you before you came
We couldn't wait for our lives to change
Such a cherished gift to your mom and dad
We'll always care for you the very best we can
We're overwhelmed . . .
We're overwhelmed . . .

Chorus

With her baby's breath upon my face
My heart swells with joy when I hear her name
When I see the likeness of her mom and me
I am overwhelmed by the mystery—
How the love of a man and wife
With God's touch brings such precious life
I'm overwhelmed . . .
I'm overwhelmed . . .

Bridge

Take my hand, Daddy dance with me
Teach me what true love really means
Teach me, Mommy without a doubt
That beauty starts from the inside out

I'm so thankful my parents are the two of you
I hope one day you'll know and you'll see in me too . . .
That I'm overwhelmed . . .
I'm overwhelmed by your love for me
I'm overwhelmed that we're a family
That I belong to you and you to me . . .

A priceless gift . . .
. . . For all to see—
We're overwhelmed . . .

Verse 3

We want so much for our little girl
Just your presence here has changed the world
From your jet dark hair and shiny twinkling eyes
To your angel lips, fingers, toes and sighs . . .

Chorus

I'm forever
For always
Will remember
I'm overwhelmed . . .
We're overwhelmed . . .

CHAPTER 17

Lenox Industrial Tools 300
New Hampshire International Speedway

July 1, 2007

*W*ell rules are rules, and when it comes to NASCAR, rules are **NOT** made to be broken! Even if you don't think you are break-ing a rule and you happen to be, look out! The axe is coming! Last week, both the cars of Jeff and Jimmie were found with an infrac-tion on the new COT car. Strange thing is, the NASCAR template still fit just fine, so the "Hendrick boys" thought they were allowed to work in the area between the templates on top of the front fenders. They thought it was an "allowed" gray area. Well, they thought wrong, and were issued no grace by NASCAR! None! Nada! Zip! Their punishments were: They were not allowed to partake in Friday's practice, were not allowed to qualify and had to start in the back of the line for the race—Jeff 41st and Jimmie 42nd! And to add to the misery, each of their crew chiefs are suspended for the next six weeks! They are each docked 100 driver and owner points AND, (I almost forgot!) Steve and Chad had to pay a little $100,000.00 fine to boot! Well, if you are a Jeff or Jimmie fan, can I just tell you, you **weren't happy!** And to hear "people" accuse them of cheating made *the blood boil, let me tell you! Jeff Meendering would now assume position as Jeff's crew chief in Steve's place for the next six weeks. (That job, along with the President of the United States, I would not wish on anyone!) But that 24-team is just that—a **TEAM!** They work together like nobody's business and our driver was incredible! He drove that car from 41ˢᵗ all the way to second place, and almost won this race! (No driver has ever won here from further back than the 13ᵗʰ starting position!) In the 24/48 shop there is a large sign that states: "Teamwork is the fuel that allows common people to attain uncommon results." We have certainly seen this today! We have also seen that*

"Teamwork is working together—even when apart!"

The fireworks have begun long before July 4ᵗʰ,
With a "pyrotechnic display" NASCAR fiercely brought forth!

The sparks began to fly with Jeff's Sonoma infraction,
And exploded into penalties causing blinding reaction!

100 points docked?
No crew chief for six weeks?

Seems like a warning would be sufficient,
Instead the jugular vein was seeked!

Oh, and a 100-grand fine for Letarte to pay up!
But he'll get it all back once our Jeff wins The Cup!

Ya seek a little independence in this "land of the free,"
Then the "iron curtain" of NASCAR
Crushes all your hopes and dreams!

But all is not lost; HMS is the "Home of the brave!"
The 24 will go on! Let your Gordon flag wave!

The broad flames of our bright Star,
Through this perilous fight,

Will shine brightly through the cloud
Of the "rocket red glare" from my eyes!

The "bursting bombs" of penalty
Will quickly disperse!

When the "winds of change" display team triumph,
For better or for worse!

So bring all your tired, your weak and your strong!
Your eyes will see the glory; the 24-team is marching on!

So over hill, over dale, time to hit the one-mile trail!
Time to warm up those tires and get that COT car to sail!

This cold, cloudy day in New Hampshire today,
Can't squelch the burning desire
To prove a win is underway!

So Jeff rolls off eighth, with Blaney on the pole,
The sound of forty-three engines
Sends a shiver through every soul!

An early CAUTION on lap 4, Ward's car blew up already!
The 24 is loose, but Jeff adapts and holds her steady!

Lap 16 he soars by Earnhardt,
(His future teammate, but not yet!)

Third is next on Jeff's agenda,
Then two more and he'll be set!

Jeff took the lead methodically,
Engulfed each enemy one by one!

He pulled away from the battlefield,
And by lap 38 is two seconds out front!

Though lap 47 displays he's 'bout as loose as it gets,
His 2½-second lead blasts the competition with his jets!

He starts lapping the field by lap 53!
Charging hard through the traffic
Saying, "move over, please!"

It's time for adjustments; GREEN pit stops are next!
The crew's work is excessive trying not to render a hex!

Now Jr.'s in the lead, then Jeff then The 2,
The next stop is on 95 to adjust; he's still loose!

He rolls off fourth right after the pit,
Wow, the pole-sitter's behind, way back in 25th!

The adjustments were wrong, now he's tight in the middle!
Lap 120's CAUTION will help, we'll modify just a little!

Newman "got hosed" as he left his pit stop——
The air came along with him; he's now in 27th spot!

Gordon starts to go backwards, again, he's **still loose**!
Then with dauntless resoluteness,
Passes Burton and Jimmie, too!

He's still in fifth place, this battle's not over!
Meendering works hard, and Steve's notes, he pours over!

Please make the right call for the 191 PIT!
Jeff G. and Jeff M. join forces with grit!

Carl Edwards was second, but ran into big trouble,
A 48-second stop can really "burst your bubble!"

Those two DEI guys are brawling for first!
Truex takes the lead and Jr. slips back to third!

Jeff's in fourth waging war with The 8 and The 5!
Goes to third on 215, looking strong and alive!

On 270, Meendering announces to Jeff,
"There's 30 laps to go;" "Go get 'em," he said!

(*If I see one more commercial, or another Aflac duck,*
I'm gonna do something drastic,
But for now, guess I'm stuck!)

With 6 laps to go, Jeff conquers Truex for second!
He hunts his next prey; it's that Denny in Car 11!

The battle is hard, with blood, sweat and gears!
My intestinal knots almost bring me to tears!

You can beat that "youngling" who thinks you're a cheat!
Show him who's Boss, I think his words now he'll eat!

They clash side by side, each pursuing the win!
Jeff could have "let him have it" and sent him for a spin!

But Jeff raced him clean for a hard-fought second place!
One more lap or two, and he would have had this race!

So Hamlin's the victor, but our guy's still The Champ!
This pageant will continue, Daytona's the next Act!

The fireworks will proceed in the hot, sunny south!
I wish I could be there, but I'll watch from my couch!

Though almost three hours away,
I'll listen for thunderous applause!
When Jeff takes the win after laying down the law!

So let freedom ring, but ignore your independence!
It's teamwork that renders results like this,
Regardless of consequences!

We all learn from our mistakes,
They make us stronger in the end!

The 24-team learned the hard way,
That on each other they can depend!

That DuPont Chevy will be worked on,
'Til the crew is manically insane!

To pass inspection perfection,
And get that 24 to Victory Lane!

CHAPTER 18

Pepsi 400
Daytona International Speedway

July 7, 2007

This sure turned out to be an interesting weekend! My husband was out riding his bike on Saturday, (long before the Pepsi 400, of course!) and he called me from the cell phone stating that he had just found a kitten, and I should come and get it, as it kept trying to get in the highway he was riding next to! Well, of course, I hopped in our van and was off to the rescue! When I showed up to his location, however, he was holding not one, but TWO precious, wiggly kittens! I said to him, "I thought there was one kitten?" And he said, "There was, but another one came out of the bushes after I talked to you!" So, he put the tiny, skinny, precious little things in the van and off I went back home. Trying to drive with two little kittens climbing on your dashboard, lap, back and all over the place was interesting, to say the least! When we arrived home, I immediately gave the famished little guys some food and water, and they were so grateful! They purred like crazy thanking me! They sure were adorable! Well, to make a long story short, we tried desperately to find homes for them, sent out e-mails, made phone calls, "the whole shebang." But . . . no takers. There was no way I could just dump them off at an animal shelter either! What if they got split up? What if they didn't get good homes? What if they were locked in a cage for weeks on end before getting adopted out? I was a wreck with worry about these poor, innocent creatures that came so very close to getting smeared into the pavement had my husband not found them! I am an animal lover to the hilt, and trust me when I tell you, it is a curse! My heart has been broken (along with my wallet!) countless times over animals! Well, I'm happy to report that the two little guys found an EXCELLENT home! **OURS!** *These "free" kittens have cost us hundreds of dollars in vet bills, but it has been worth it! What a joy they are and a riot to watch play together! They each have such unique personalities, too! We were going to name them "Duey" and "Monte," short for "DuPont" and "Monte Carlo!" (Hmmm, I wonder where I got that idea?!) Duey's name stuck, but Monte's was changed to "Stewart!" The reason for this change is that he is orange and white and always causing trouble! Always slapping his brother up-side the head and picking a fight with him! (Don't worry, it's all in love, he won't be needing any anger management classes!) Plus, he climbs everything! SO, you can probably guess why the name fit! So! "Duey" and "Stewy" are the latest additions to the Bennett family! Even though I am really not a "cat person," it is just sick how much I love these little guys! They love us, too, so it's a regular lovefest around here! As Martha Stewart would say: (No relation to my "Stewart" by the way!)*

"It's a good thing!"

There's an assembly of carcasses
Sun burnt and crisp,

With muggy, oppressive humidity
Causing sweat-beaded lips!

They'd rather be here midst this boiling mosh,
Than basking by the surf or chillin' with Palm Beacher's "Posh!"

Pepsi 400

They'll cope with the heat (And believe me, it's HOT!
I know, 'cuz I live here; you can sweat like a hog!)

But hour after hour a chill will run through their bones,
As they cheer on their driver to bring the *big trophy* home!

The track's as hot and greasy as the fries in the concession!
And the guy on the pole is about to teach a few lessons!

He's among the elite that have won at this joint!
He's as cool as a cucumber, ready to make a fine point!

Others look to him, 'cuz they know he's the Ace!
With Daytona prizes, his trophy case is laced!

With the explosive call to GREEN
By the raucous Kevin James . . .

. . . I thought a self-induced aneurysm
Would surely take place!

A day–to-night grind begins at full throttle!
Time to maneuver those Goodyears,
There's no time to dawdle!

Jeff grabs the first points for leading already!
But the forty-two behind are intense, brisk and heady!

There's proof to this notion . . .
. . . There's a YELLOW on lap 3!

Jeff's tight and unyielding,
The center needs to be free!

A big wreck on 14, involving Hamlin and Stewart!
With nowhere to go, Jr. and Sorensen add to it!

Another CAUTION on 21, and I've got something to say . . .
. . . Thanks for asking my opinion;
I'm glad to share it today!——

I'm against the impound races,
For many reasons "under the sun!"
With today's safety concerns, why do we even have one?!

Is it safe to start a restrictor plate race
With poor handling cars?

With some ending up in the wall
Where they could acquire great harm?!

Or take out the innocent, prepared for the day?
What if Jeff was a recipient and caught up in the fray?!

Yes, it's a bad idea, in my *humble* opinion,
Not that you care, just thought I'd throw that in!

Let's see, now where were we . . .
On lap 30's a new leader,
It's Jamie McMurray, but below the yellow line he teetered!

He's black-flagged and now will be sent to the back,
Clint Bowyer takes his place out in front of the pack.

Jeff's been real tight since we started this thing,
The crew's sweatin' bullets trying to make that car sing!

Pepsi 400

More CAUTIONS flew for one reason or another!
From tight and loose conditions,
Jeff's team strives to recover!

We're up to lap 94 and could use another Caution,
To work on the 24-machine, as it's just shy of awesome!

He's hung about mid-pack for most of this race,
Even stalled in his pit, but never lost his "game-face!"

Sterling blew a tire on lap 94,
Took Gilliland with him, and there was a CAUTION once more!

There are 41 laps to go and Jeff's in sixteenth,
By lap 124, he's cruised up to eighth!

Lap 125, he goes from seventh to fifth!
Look out boys, "Big Daddy's" "on the stick!"

He goes from fifth to ninth
Just when everything looked as it should!
More adjustments on 131, Come on make it good!

I'm chompin' on my gum now at turbulent pace!
Jeff's 3-wide on the outside, in a very crammed space!

Rationing real estate at 200 miles an hour!
That kind of negotiating would make the normal guy cower!

He goes from eighth to forth in one measly lap!
Then a CAUTION on 143, now fifth is where he's at!

Now Casey's at the helm. His teammate, Jeff is in fourth!
Just when momentum gets rockin',

There's another CAUTION,
Of course!

It's now lap 150, and *who's in the primo position?*
No matter by luck, skill, chance or attrition!

"WAKE UP PEOPLE," Let Pepsi Max quench your thirst!
There's only **FIVE laps to go** and Jeff Gordon's in **FIRST!**

Casey pushes from behind, looks like a win's in the bag!
I'm now aging by the nanosecond, morphing into a hag!

Then Jeff loses Casey's draft and falls to the outside!
It looks like it's over, with no help in sight!!

But he pulls off a great finish and ends up in fifth!
Personally, I'm completely spent and at the end of my wits!

. . . I thought for sure he'd fall in behind a very loose Kyle,
And just nudge him a little, and move him with style!

McMurray fought back from a black flag to the checkers,
A great points day for Jeff with no call to the "wreckers!"

McMurray got the win by the "skin of his teeth!"
With Kyle just five-one-thousandths beneath!

The 2 was in third, next Edwards then Jeff,
Mears ended eighteenth and Jimmie in tenth.

But if you're "lookin' for adventure,"
Just "Head out on the highway!"

"Get your motor runnin'."
A CHICAGO WIN IS COMIN' OUR WAY!

132

CHAPTER 19

USG Sheetrock 400
Chicagoland Speedway

July 15, 2007

O.K., I've had my precious little kittens for a week now, and it's unbelievable how much time they steal from me! I might as well have two toddlers running around! It's taken me about three times longer to write this re-cap because they keep jumping up and playing on my desk and keyboard! They also try and attack the moving characters on the screen! My all-time favorite "adventure" is when one of them comes out of nowhere, jumps up and hangs on my back, claws dug deep within my dermis, and continues to scale up to my neck where he decides to curl up and take a nap! Besides my shredded, bleeding back, it's absolutely precious! ☺ Oh, to have nothing to do but play, eat and sleep and be loved! One day, in Heaven, but not today!

Back to work!

A devastating fire charred the Windy City,
So many years ago.

But doesn't compare to our fiery, smoke-free auto,
That's blown in to really "stink up the show!"

When that Nicorette machine is in your rearview mirror,
A mental melt down soon will take over!

Jeff wants to win here again, like he did last year,
So don't get burnt, boy, you'd better move over!

So let's get started, our players are set,
For our Romeo racer to try and woo Joliet!

Hansen sings the Anthem with harmonious panache,
While those cool F-18's fly with their tail hooks locked!

This domain has cheered the Bears, the Bulls and the Cubs,
But a "different animal" today, draws a crowd to this hub!

Jeff's teammate, Casey, starts off in the lead,
Until Truex steals it away——on lap 6 was this deed.

The 24's really loose, but still takes his chances!
By lap 68, he takes fifth and advances.

He's by Kyle for fourth on lap 106,
And nearly crashes with someone on his 111 GREEN PIT!

. . . "7's" were unlucky; The 07 was too fast,
Then The 7 missed the commitment cone——
He was too hard on the gas!

The adjustments weren't good; Gordon's out sideways loose!
Jeff's twelve seconds behind
And seems to be hung without a noose!

USG Sheetrock 400

Lap 154 demonstrates a YELLOW again——
Last race winner's right front blew Jamie straight to the fence!

Stewart assumes the lead,
Jimmie tags behind in second,
Kyle's in fourth, Mears is eighth and Jeff's up in seventh!

Those Hendrick boys are cruisin'
Midst the gaggles all over the track,
Until Jeff slips to fourteenth and is descending to the back!

A lap 201 CAUTION allows some 24-car mechanics!
He's twelfth of 18 lead-lappers, but we'll try not to panic!

Jimmie's hard in the wall; his right rear had let go!
This lap 222 debacle really messed up his goal!

The remaining laps divulged CAUTIONS
And battles for positions!

We advanced to ninth place
With luck, drudge and attrition!

To pull off another top 10,
Considering the state of that 24-car,

Is something to be thankful for,
Plus the points added thus far!

Stewart smoked the field——
That's hard for a Gordon fan to swallow!

But in our frustration and despondence,
We won't tarry, nor will wallow!

Though Gordon didn't win the heart of Joliet this week,
He'll soon be "romancing the stone," and kissing the bricks
For that rock-solid win that he'll seek!

So roll out the red carpet, Indy, your boy's coming home!
Alert your friends and neighbors,
Charge up your NEXTEL phone!

The Pittsboro Champ will soon be rolling in!
Get ready to proclaim a fifth Brickyard win!!

CHAPTER 20

Allstate 400 at the Brickyard
Indianapolis Motor Speedway

July 29, 2007

O.K., so I guess we'll let Stewart have a win once in a while! (So long as it doesn't happen again!) I thought Jeff was going to take the win this week, but then again, don't I think that every week?! ☺ I have to sing tomorrow for a big, week-long State FBI convention. It's good to have friends in high places! I'm either going to feel really safe in a room full of FBI agents, or really targeted! I'll let you know how it turned out! (Pending I live to tell about it!) I hope I live to tell about it, because I have to go back and sing again Thursday night! Tomorrow I'm opening with our National Anthem, and Thursday will be Celine Dion's rendition (turned Maria Bennett's rendition!) of God Bless America. I just love those two songs, and as often as I sing them, I never tire of them. I am so very proud and blessed to be living in this great country! Don't ever take your freedoms for granted! God **has** blessed America! In countless ways! And in my "humble opinion,"
I think it's time America blessed God!

There are lots of "Who's" in "Hoosierville,"
. . . 43 are the qualified picks.

Whose biggest dream in the Heartland today,
Is to *smooch* some gritty, sun-baked bricks!

The greatest "Who" in "Hoosierville"
Has puckered at this hallowed ground before!

Four times to be exact, and it must have been good,
Because today he's come back for some more!

To some he's the "Grinch" who stole the wins from so many,
To others he's the "Who's Who" among racers!

But regardless of your thoughts,
He's one of Indy's great icons,
In pro sports from the Colts to the Pacers!

He cut his "racing teeth" in Indy,
When he was just a mere lad;

Was wisely brought to this state
By his mom and Bickford, his dad!

Guided, encouraged and *schlepped* to countless races,
Made this "rising son" the star he is today . . .
. . . One of NASCAR's most recognized faces!

He won the inaugural Cup race at this historical place,
A fete only Jeff Gordon can claim!

This "Pittsboro Prince" is back home again,
We hope what's engraved in the trophy is his name!

But we've got a long way to go in this *Allstate 400*—
I feel the 24-team is in "good hands!"

We'll see what he's got; the fans are going crazy!
All 250,000 in the stands!

The surrounding agriculture is growing,
Along with our anticipation!
I'm thinkin' it's time we harvested a win!

So Jeff will plow through the field
And weed out the rubble
From that 21st spot he starts in!

The youngest driver's on the pole,
You know Sorensen is stoked . . .

. . . To think his Qualifying run
Had so many veterans smoked!

However ironic, he's the one leading the others,
And is feeling like "King of the Road!"

But he better watch his back
and hold the peddle to the metal,
'Cuz some folks behind him are beginning to unload!

The 24, for one, has picked up ten spots in eight laps!
Then Jeff Green hits the wall on lap 14!

No need for a competition YELLOW,
That was on the schedule to be thrown,
At next loop around on number 15!

The 11 was caught speeding,
HOW SAD AM I ! **(NOT!)**
I'll play him a "pinky violin" tune!

Jeff's out in ninth and I expect more quick advances,
And him contending for first spot rather soon!

A BIG WRECK on lap 20!
Newman had trouble,
Just after Dale Jr. took the lead!

The debris field is monstrous!
Looks like it will be quite a while,
Before the remaining wheels can get up to speed!

On lap 45, Jeff takes third from Montoya,
Then another colossal crack-up emerges!

Almost a four-wide wad going into turn 4,
Doesn't work, and seven cars receive scourges!

Jimmie Johnson is done, for him this race won't be won.
He and the others hit like the ton of bricks
Buried beneath them!

Truex was penalized, for speeding again,
He ignored the stop paddle, now behind him!

We restart on 52, then another CAUTION on 54!
Looks like a good day to have car insurance
At the Allstate 400!

We'll try and restart again, on lap 58
Until lap 60 finds **another YELLOW** we're under!

More bad luck for Jimmie,
He slams the wall hard!
The inferno singed the lashes off his face!

Jeff went in third and came out in eighteenth!
Many stayed out to gain positions in this race!

What's this on 67? Hamlin trying to block our Jeff?!
Is this boy trying to mess with our man?!

As the heat begins to build, just beneath my collar,
Jeff takes twelfth away and claims Denny's land!

The 24 is by Stremme for seventh position,
By lap number 82.

There's a battle between Truex, Kyle and Jeff,
As they play a little game of "switcheroo!"

Jeff's out eleventh after a debris CAUTION on 89,
But his car's too tight in traffic; it won't work there real fine!

It's clean air we crave; He's by "The Biff" for fifth position,
Inching closer and closer ·
To laundered atmospheric conditions!

There's a 109 duel for the two upfront drivers . . .
. . . The 29 and Stewart fight for the lead!

Then the wall meets the bulls-eye
On that Target car of Stremme.
Jeff's fourth with 31 laps to filch the lead!

On lap 36, The 8-car blew up,
To the dismay of Jr.'s personal nation!

Kyle decided to pit, now our 24's in third place,
Stay put and leave the "tube" on this station!

Only 12 laps to go, Stewart's knocking on Kevin's door,
He wants to win for the second week in a row!

Does he think he's our Jeff? Must he copy his success?
Jeff's supposed to win today, doesn't he know?!

Harvick loses his spot; Jeff goes by him for third,
I'm assuming Kevin's plan wasn't to go backwards!

Montoya's in second, and our "Always a Winner" hangs on,
And finds a great finish, a top five up in third!

So Tony takes the win, and for this I am sick!
Must we be subjected to more of his fence-climbing shtick?

Kyle made it back and ended up in fourth!
Our young pole-sitter's fifth, riding high on his horse!

But Pocono is comin', and make no mistake——
Our birthday boy will win and take the whole cake!

His gift will be wrapped in a glistening trophy,
A celebration in Victory lane with little Ella "Sofie!"

I'm proud to be a fan of such a hard-working guy,
And equally diligent team working together, side-by-side!

Keep up the pace, boys! *Rock on* to the end!
The Waldorf awaits **THE BEST OF THE BEST!!**

CHAPTER 21

Pennsylvania 500
Pocono Raceway

August 5, 2007

If you've ever been to a race at Pocono Raceway before, you know exactly what I mean when I say, "comin' around the mountain!" I never thought that long, winding, rough road would ever end! What an incredible climb! Then, when you reach the top, plopped right in the middle of nowhere is Pocono Raceway! I enjoyed the "trip up," however. Even in the slow parade of bumper-to-bumper traffic and no McDonalds in sight, it was so exciting to know you were all headed to the same place and all couldn't wait to get there! It was cool to see all the fans' homes along the way decked with their favorite driver's flag and other racing paraphernalia! Of course, every "Jeff Gordon home" deserved a few good honks of the horn! Arriving at the speedway, you see acre after acre of thousands of people! It's just a blast! It's fun to "spar" with those folks who are fans of "other" drivers other than Jeff! Bring it on, people! ☺ It's too bad Jeff couldn't take the win this week on his birthday weekend! And, you know that FBI convention I told you I sang at last week? (Obviously, I survived!) I'm thinking of hiring one of my "new friends" and finding out just what in the world Kurt Busch was doing differently than every-

body else!? Maybe he has "friends in high places," too! Like NASA, maybe?! Nah, I guess not. The "FBI of NASCAR" would have found out for sure!

**As we know, they are VERY particular
about playing by their rules!**

130,000 fans are "comin' around the mountain" today,
Through the winding roads of those Pocono "hills."
Driver flags on the homes lead the way!

They know the slow climb on this rangy road is tough,
But is worth risking the life of their brakes and the clutch!

"Six white horses" might be easier for this treacherous climb,
The conquest must be worth it! 130,000 don't lie!

They arrive at the destined, appointed place,
And get their sites and their snacks all arranged for the race!

Jr.'s on the pole, and ready to pursue,
He hasn't been there in a while—since 2002!

Chris Tucker's the Grand Marshall, and yells the familiar call,
Then "Rush Hour" begins, until McMurray thwacks the wall!

Jeff started in eleventh, but now he's in tenth,
In hot pursuit of a sweep, and tries to avoid the hard fence!

He steadily advances and begins to conquer the field,
By lap 13, he's sixth and soon fifth place Jimmie will yield!

Lap 29's GREEN PIT stop was no adjustments, just four tires,
The car's running good, but the brakes are starting to expire!

"Oy Vay," I say, you've got to be kidding, not again!
And to top it all off, the 2-car is **eight seconds ahead!!!!**

Kurt's getting even stronger?! How can he be going so fast?
Has Sunoco been replaced by some kind of rocket-fuel gas?

The DEBRIS CAUTION on 53
Allows Team 24 to work on the brakes,

I think, "Get more air to those 'puppies,'
There's too much at stake!"

Lap 78, Jeff's by Earnhardt, and swipes the fourth spot,
And inches closer to Newman;
Attempting to show what he's got!

By lap 97, he's up in third behind Denny!
Busch is still leading, but Jeff's on fire with that Chevy!

The 24's up to second by lap 108,
If he could just get to first, it would just make my day!

The CAUTION is out on lap 122,
The right front on The 8 car spun him out 'cuz it blew!

The restart shows Newman nipping hard at Jeff's tail,
Stewart dogs them both, then by Jeff they both sail!

Greg Biffle's spin brings out lap 137's CAUTION.
Time to put the air pressures up
And make that DuPont car more awesome!

Lap 145, Dale Jr. takes the point,
Even after spinning earlier, here at this joint!

(ESPN's doing fine with their coverage so far,
But please, must they keep demo'ing
The computerized draft on the cars?——

. . . I know technology is fun, (My cell phone's a blast!)
But a repetitious display will wear out really fast!!)

Jeff's up to third by lap 155!
If he could make it to the lead, it would truly save my life!

So close yet so far; I'd really love Jeff to sweep!
Especially on his birthday weekend,
The trophy's the gift that he seeks!

There's a couple more CAUTIONS,
Some mishaps and wrecks,
Seems the "racing" under YELLOW just doesn't seem to end!

We're on lap 198, SO CLOSE TO THE END!
Jeff's in fourth behind Denny, but by only 3 tenths!

There's not enough time, so in fourth place he'll stay,
Overall a top five is not a bad day!

Kurt Busch gets his first victory in 51 races,
He was like a runaway train never slowing his paces!!

Jr. is second, with Hamlin in third,
Jimmie Johnson in fifth, and check it out! Oh my word!

. . . All Hendrick cars ended up in the top ten,
Way to go boys! You've done it again!

O.K., "Mr. Gordon," it's time for a win!
Watkins Glen is the place we hope FIRST PLACE
You'll end in!

. . . I can feel it in my bones, way down to my toes!
Can't wait to watch the action and the drama unfold!

I lived in Watkins Glen——a fun, quaint little town!
But it's really fun when Jeff wins,
And I can cheer proudly out loud!

Just remember who you are; you're the road course Champ!
Know your friends and fans
Are totally "juiced up" and "amp'd!"

Cross the finish line first, **WE KNOW YOU CAN DO IT!!!**
Just please watch your back
And stay away from Tony Stewart!

CHAPTER 22

Centurion Boats at the Glen
Watkins Glen International Speedway

August 12, 2007

*W*atkins Glen. Just saying those words floods my soul with count-less memories of my childhood! I was fortunate enough to grow up in this part of the country for most of my early years until we moved an hour away in my tenth grade year of high school. I love it when the race is here every August, and the camera pans around and shows beautiful, scenic shots of my old stomping grounds! Now living down here in Florida, a "pinge" of homesickness comes over me when I see those beautiful, rolling hills! (Then I remember the frigid, icy winters and I'm all-better!) Years ago, my then boyfriend, Marty, (Now, my husband!) took me to a race up at the Glen. Al-though not a NASCAR race back then, I remember like it was yes-terday, walking up a dirt road towards the track, when all of a sud-den, the loud scream of racecar engines enveloped me like the cloud that swarms Pig Pen on Charlie Brown! I'm telling you, a surge went straight to my veins, and obviously, has never left! This was also the place where my mom "got hooked" on NASCAR! My aunt and uncle brought my folks to a race there, and it was a year where Jeff Gordon won! My mom said to herself, "My, that young man's

quite good!" My aunt, who is **not** a Jeff Gordon fan (Can you believe it?!) said to her, "Oh, Sissy, you don't want to root for him, **he wins all the time!"** Mom tuned in to the races from that day forward and learned just how often he did win! AND, she had the smarts to make Jeff Gordon her driver . . . in spite of my Aunt!
    Ya know, some things just aren't worth arguing about!

Ninety laps of twists and turns,
High-speed racing 'round this winding worm!

Jeff's on the poll due to our *downpour friend*,
——The position he deserves at the very end!

The history at The Glen extends farther than you know!
It's my childhood home, and a place I well know!

So many summers I spent climbing the great Glen;
And it's here I caught "the fever"
That from my veins has never left!

The first time I stepped foot
On these rough and sacred grounds,

A rush came over my mortal chassis
From those distant engine sounds!

I felt myself break out in a fever and chill,
And my love for the sport of racing
Was immediately instilled!

The sleepy little Italian town
At the southern tip of Seneca Lake,

Was suddenly jolted into big-time action
When The Cup boys roused it awake!

Jeff's won four times at this particular place,
We're all poised and ready for him to take a fifth race!

My Track Pass is tuned in, my pen's ready to take notes!
Some caramel cream Pepsi Jazz
Bubbles swiftly down my throat!

The GREEN flag is thrown; Kenseth steals Jeff's lead fast;
But Jeff retrieves it in the inner loop—
WE'LL HAVE NONE OF THAT!

His lap times are faster than he's run here all week!
He leads Hamlin and Stewart with almost a 2-second lead!

There's a CAUTION on lap 10,
The "kitty litter" absorbs The 12!

David Ragan follows and is axle-deep in the gravelly swells!

Jeff missed the restart and Stewart took away first!
Anyone leading but The 24-car, to me is simply the worst!

Lap 16 reports that Kevin Harvick's losing his brakes.
Vickers spins on 22 after gaining sixteen spots in this race!

The 24 pits due to a CAUTION once more;
The team puts one round in the right rear,
And as for tires, he took four.

Jeff's first off pit road! Time to reclaim the top space!
He starts to buzz by the first seven,
Who stayed out to gain spots in this race.

By lap 31, French newcomer, Carpentier leads.
Jeff's coming in a hurry, but the wrong guy took the lead!

It's Stewart again! Then Jeff, then The 8 . . .
. . . The competition continues with Hamlin then The 48!

My anxiety rises; my bones are filled with stress!
If I only had an "easy button" right now I could compress!

Then lap 44 was truly a happy moment for me!
Stewart spins in turn 1 and Jeff assumed the lead!

A CAUTION abounds on lap fifty-two,
Reed Sorensen spins and Montoya does too!

Jeff's off pit road first, beating Earnhardt by inches,
But resides fifth in line due to the top four "non-pitters!"

The 24 leads again, by lap 60, once more!
Only 30 laps to go, but his fuel's five laps too short!

Turn one claims more victims over and over again;
Earnhardt and Petty lost engines . . . and then . . . !

. . . A restart wreck on 72 causes a "ruckus" on the track!
The 29 and Montoya "lock horns" about the flack!

Face to face and helmet to helmet,
Their "discussion" ensued!

All this pushin' and shovin' will surely make the news!

There's mess and engine fluid all over the place!
A RED flag is thrown, bringing a halt to this race!

The cars were parked and waiting,
When a Kenseth fan hopped the fence!!

Carrying his nerve and his Sharpie
To Kenseth's window, no less!

Can you imagine Matt sitting there,
Minding his own business?

When a half-clad, inebriated fan peeks in,
Seeking autograph wishes?!

The authorities took over this deranged, erratic show!
Then the cars finally re-fired, with 15 laps to go!

Jeff's in the lead and he's pulling away!
When a killer CAUTION comes out and bunches up the fray!

Eight laps to go, Jeff's restart was great!
I'm holding my breath, the win's 5 laps away!

The 6 spins and lays all kinds of gravel on the track!
Which ads to my hysteria; my sanity's under attack!

With Stewart all over Jeff's bumper like *white on rice*,
I pray that he'll find manners and be really nice!

Less than two laps to go, and who just took a spin?!
THAT WICKED TURN ONE MAKES JEFF LOSE THE WIN!

I'm outraged and vexed, and physically sick!
I'm so mad right now, I could eat a log and spit toothpicks!

The paint drips off my walls
From radioactive heat from my head!

A ninth place finish for Jeff,
When it should have been a win instead!!!

I seethe the rest of the evening,
Unable to speak!
I know it's "just racing" but this situation is unique!

If I know Jeff's *vibe*, he's hopping mad too!
That notion will carry him right to a Michigan win for his crew!

Though I feel like someone licked the red
Off my proverbial lollipop,

I expect those DuPont flames to fire forward,
With winning fervor that just won't stop!

CHAPTER 23

3M Performance 400
Michigan International Speedway

August 21, 2007

*W*ell, after six long weeks off due to the penalty issued by NASCAR back at Infineon, Steve Letarte is back on top of the Pit box in his crew chief chair! What an incredible job Jeff Meendering did in his place the past six weeks! Way to go, Jeff M.! Hope you enjoy my little song at the beginning of this re-cap in celebration of Steve's return! (Sing to the tune of "My Boyfriend's Back.") Thought I'd have a little fun with the event! ☺ After two rain delays, we finally were able to get this race in, but not until Tuesday! (My husband took a half-day off work to come home for the race!) Then, after waiting out two delays, we had to wait a little longer for the fog to lift! I feel badly for the folks who had tickets to this race! This event had many ups and downs, as you will read about. Unfortunately for Steve, his first week back after his "vacation" ended in a "down." If it weren't so stressful trying to gain bonus points for the start of the Chase, it wouldn't be that big of a deal! Congratulations to Kurt Busch, who once again, had nitrous oxide in his gas tank! (O.K., what's going on here?!) Maybe Steve's just a little "rusty." After all, we have had a lot of rain!

I'm not worried, we'll be back . . . you'll see!

Our crew chief's back and you're gonna be in trouble!
(Hey la, hey la, our crew chief's back!)

When you see him comin', better cut out on the double!
(Hey la, hey la, our crew chief's back!)

Gordon's on the pole and he's comin' after you!
(Hey la, hey la, our crew chief's back!)

Steve's rested up and ready and he knows just what to do!
(Hey la, hey la, our crew chief's back!)

Hey! Meendering's been tryin'!
Yes! He's really good, we sure ain't lyin'!

Letarte's been gone for such a long time!
(Hey la, hey la, our crew chief's back!)

Now he's back and things will be fine.
(Hey la, hey la, our crew chief's back!)

You're gonna be sorry when you see that Chevy soar!
(Hey la, hey la, our crew chief's back!)

He'll execute the strategy cooked up while he was bored!
(Hey la, hey la, our crew chief's back!)

Hey! You know he wasn't cheatin'!
Now, the field will get a beatin'!

Our crew chief's back, he'll maintain Jeff's reputation!
(Hey la, hey la, our crew chief's back!)

The other drivers might as well just take a
Permanent vacation!
(Hey la, hey la, our crew chief's back!)

Hey! The team's united and they're comin'!
Now, you better start a runnin'!

Wait and see!

Hey la, hey la, **OUR CREW CHIEF'S BACK!**

* * * * *

O.K, folks, you've had enough of the '60s, now back to 2007!
Time to take advantage of the break
In that deluge from the heavens!

It's not Sunday or Monday, but it's Tuesday, my friend!
We're finally ready to race; *happy days* are here again!

It's the "dawning of a new error," this early *Tuesday* morn,
We'll have "breakfast with the champion,"
When this fog elevates some more!

It will be a GREEN/YELLOW start to this Michigan race,
When the spotters have clear view,
We'll really pick up the pace!

But just when we thought the wait was finally over,
Lap 9 sends the cars to park 'cuz the RED FLAG took over!

The drivers and teams hang out in the pits,
There's nothing to do; the fog is dangerously thick!

NASCAR officials block the cars from their crews . . .
. . . Like a white army of *storm troopers*
With an *Empire* mission to pursue!

Biffle swiped Jeff's lead when we went GREEN once again,
Then "Juan *Problem* Montoya" took an aero loose spin!

Jeff radios to Steve that the car is *fit as a fiddle*,
Except it won't rotate well 'cuz it's too tight in the middle!

There's a COMPETITION CAUTION on lap 31,
Jeff makes a two-tire stop and is out number one!

Robby Gordon didn't pit so he had a brief lead——
Why he did this? No clue! It's no way to gain speed!

His crew chief was baffled, he didn't even know why . . .
Then Robby made a GREEN stop, probably wanting to cry!

Johnson assumed the lead on lap 47,
Jeff's losing positions to Vickers and Kenseth!

He cries out to Steve,
"My car's never been this tight here before!"
As he continues to get passed, it's obvious Jeff's in a war!

He holds on in eighth while Vickers has the lead!
I need a Rapid Release Tylenol to give me relief!!

The front still needs emancipating, after receiving four tires,
But the rear feels as though it's hanging on by a wire!

"This ain't working," Jeff said,
Then just in time there's a CAUTION!

The crew goes to work,
Jeff gains six spots, **now that's awesome!**

This race is about half done,
And Jeff's up in fifth!

Then on lap 101 The 2's on top of the list!
The 17's in second; Jeff's by Vickers for fourth!

Next victim is Jimmie,
Jeff takes third place, of course!

That spot is short-lived!
Gordon's by Kenseth for second!

My spirits are lifted,
Then shot down the next second!

At 55 laps to go, Jeff's 2½ seconds behind Kurt!
But his rear "shark fin" is loose, taking time to fix it will hurt!

Lap 164 shows Jeff 5½ seconds behind the leader!
It's here at this point that my nerves begin to teeter!

Paul Menard "blew up" on lap 166!
Here's a ripe opportunity for The 24 to pit!

Well, that was uneventful, Jeff's out ninth and lost positions!
I'm getting desperate! Losing hope! Calling out for attrition!

Twenty-six laps to go, and Jeff's now up to seventh,
But thirteen seconds behind the leader
Is not exactly "heaven!"

But at the CAUTION on 175,
Jeff stayed out and now he's second!

He feels he's better on old tires;
The true test is ahead of him!

Then all goes south on lap 183 . . .
Jeff thinks his tire is cut and rapidly loses speed!

Thirteen to go and Jeff's tryin' not to wreck . . .
But **IT HAPPENS** on 189; I'm now not "playing with a full deck!"

He spins and ends up in the "swamp,"
Formally known as the infield!
He's stuck in the muck and to the safety crew yields!

He tried to get out of anxious Matt Kenseth's way,
But Matt was in a hurry and he didn't want to wait!

Busch wins again and sucks the wind from my sails!
Our celebration is hosed, but at Bristol we'll prevail!

A 27th place finish makes me nauseous at best!
Only three more chances for pre-Chase bonus points left!

This week *it's my party, and I'll cry if I want to!*
We're your fans, Jeff, and we suffer when you do!

But we have faith we have hope——
You just needed a break from top tens!

We'll postpone the party to Saturday
After your 6th Bristol win!

CHAPTER 24

Sharpie 500
Bristol Motor Speedway

August 25, 2007

Well, now, how about a lesson in Japanese to start off today's re-cap?! I know, you knew it was just a matter of time, right?! Ha-ha . . . I'm a home school mom, but I'm not THAT good! ☺ I did, however, use a Japanese word in today's re-cap, unbeknownst to me! It was pointed out by one of my readers on the famed Jeff Gordon Network Forum! The word is "scoche." Because I know nothing of the Japanese language, I will directly quote what JG Network member, s2d2boyd wrote to me after I posted this re-cap on the Network:

> *"Thanks, Maria! I didn't get to watch most of the Bristol race so I had no idea how he got caught a lap down until you explained it. Always enjoy your creations! For future reference, "scoche" is actually spelled "sukoshi." It's Japanese for "little" or "little bit." It IS pronounced the way you spelled it. (Not trying to be a snoot or anything. I heard my mother use that term my whole life and thought she had made it up. Then I moved to Japan and found out it was for real. I didn't know my mom knew a Japanese word!) Anyway, thanks again!"*

So! There ya have it! Isn't that interesting? Thank you, SO MUCH, s2d2boyd for enlightening us! For the record, I hardly think you are a "snoot!" I always enjoy learning and I appreciate you taking the time to teach us something new! (New to me, anyway!) Myself and the three other people who will read this book thank you! (Ha-ha)

*Well, the verbiage is not the only thing foreign around here these days! Look at the newly reconfigured Bristol Motor Speedway! Not sure if I'm sold on the "new" Bristol or not. I'll let you know . . . Another "foreign object" is the position where Jeff placed in this race! VERY out of the "norm!" He truly had some hard "luck" today. Oh well, such is life. "Ups," "Downs," and "All-arounds!" Something we ALL learn and experience on a daily basis! Jeff and his team are all humans just like the rest of us! Except **sometimes**, WE drive faster!* ☺

Anyone hungry for some Sushi?

"Thunder Valley's" turned "Tornado Alley,"
With new banking and increased grooves!

The gladiators are prepared and ready,
To test out all new moves!

The place is packed, as usual,
With the normal, sold-out crowd!

Loud screams of engines and animated fans
Make a familiar deafening sound!

Some super-hard Goodyears and the COT car to boot,
Will make the fanfare worth watching
And worth paying all that loot!

The pomp began when the MRO kids sang
Our National Anthem today,

Sharpie 500

And USA-signs blanketed proudly,
Across the crowd in patriotic display!

The pageantry continued with fireworks galore!
But the fans were still restless, only wanting some more!

They were ready to scrutinize a 500-lap test,
Of man and machine and see who'd finish best!

But for 24-fans, we know who's best already!
We have a right to brag and be a tad bit heady!

Our driver is the winningest *Bristol Beast* here!
With five wins already and for the sixth one we'll cheer!

It's not braggin' if it's true, if I do say so myself!
Just check out his "trophy case" and count 'em yourself!

Although Jeff's starting spot is less than impressive today,
He begins in eighteenth, the race lead by Kasey Kahne.

But Jeff hastens forward, advancing, looking fine!
And passes The 29 on lap . . . **29!**

By lap 53, he's by Ragan for fifth!
He's on the move now and is lookin' real slick!

He passed Juan Pablo, then Edwards for third!
(Today he needs his Nicorette car 'cuz he's smokin' for sure!)

Dale Jr. passed Jeff on lap 73,
Next is a bullring battle between Edwards and he!

They fight for position; Jeff's getting tight in the middle!
Then he flips spots with Earnhardt like hotcakes on a griddle!

Now he's up to third,
Then there's a "freak of nature" occurrence——
GREEN pit stops *at Bristol*? Usually Caution pit's flourish!

Then just as my shock ceases, on the very next lap,
There's a CAUTION on 125 when Sauter's slow on the gas!

Jeff had a good stop; some adjustments were done,
He returned to the coliseum for some action and fun!

The 1-car was posted; his crew left some loose lugs!
He's now sent to the back with some slow-running *thugs*!

LaBonte's in Jeff's sights on lap 137!
He pilfers second from Bobby like a cruel heist from a 7-11!

. . . But in this case it's legal, stealing's the right thing to do!
First place is in his sights; next it's Kasey he'll pursue!

While we're stuck on this theme,
Come on Jeff, *drive it like you stole it!*

Drive the wheels off that chassis!
Burn rubber, Baby! You own it!

Then on a lap 210 CAUTION
Hamlin's engine had a dramatic end!

With a smoky, flaming fire,
His toasted motor's a "has been!"

Another CAUTION on 225 as The 01 and 89 spin!
Jimmie helped them with this effort;
Jeff will stay out and not pit!

Sharpie 500

There's heavy communication between "Stevie" and Jeff,
They've come here to win
And will make severe adjustments next!

But to not pit was detrimental,
And that's just my observance,

But watching Jeff going backwards
Is doing him no service!

The WRONG WAY sign was posted
On the freeway in my head!
Jeff's dropping like a bomb, "The car's terrible," he said!

Now he's unlucky in seventh on lap 274!
"Hold on!" yelled his spotter on lap 304!

On lap 332, looks like the top three guys might wreck!
The 99, Jr. and Kasey are really giving each other "heck!"

GREEN-flag pits began on lap 358,
Jeff wanted to lead a lap, so he pitted really late!

If only he could have waited just a little *scoche* longer!
He wouldn't have gone a lap down,
But would have been a lot stronger!

See, the CAUTION came out right after he pit . . .
. . . It's racing moves like this that throw a fan into fits!

Now he's back in eighteenth where he started this charade.
He'll be the "lucky dog" next, which should *brighten his day!*

David Ragan spins again!
Three CAUTIONS belong to him alone!
Time to call it a day, and take that *puppy* home!

More YELLOW's abounded and on lap 451,
There's a CAUTION again when Jimmie slams Ricky Rudd!

Jeff caught a piece of the action,
Now his bumper flaps in the breeze!
Then at 10 laps to go The 24's in nineteenth!

He loses another position, and then gains it back again!
Yay, wave a flag! He's in **nineteenth** where he'll end!

Yes, I'm slightly sarcastic at this point in the game!
But if Jeff doesn't win, my demeanor's not the same!

My Office Depot friends will rub this race in my face!
Their guy, Carl Edwards wins this heinous Bristol race!

Thankfully Carl back-flips without breaking his neck!
While Gordon fans sit and sulk,
Wadded up in an emotional wreck!

The Bonus points elude us; only two chances left!
I'm *California dreamin'* where I hope he'll be best!

So as the teams traipse cross-country
To an oval that's a "D",
An "A+" awaits Jeff! Tune in and you'll see!

CHAPTER 25

Sharp AQUOS 500
California Speedway

September 2, 2007

*Well, now. Our second-to-last chance to gain valuable bonus points for the Chase, and we had another bad week for the third week in a row! And to top it all off, Jimmie Johnson swipes the bonus points! I know Brian France's goal was to make The Chase exciting, but does it have to be **this** exciting?! Jeff earned a 317-point lead during the "regular" season, and now he has to lose all of those points except for 40 of them for his four wins? Something is just not adding up here! Is there nothing to be gained for **owning** the points lead almost the entire season? Is consistency no longer prized? O.K., Mr. France, time for more tweaking and changing of this Chase format! Well, we'll see what happens! Oh, it will be exciting all right! It may put some of us over the edge, but it will be exciting! Right now, however, I need a break! Tomorrow is Labor Day, and hopefully our family can go to the beach for the first time this summer (now that summer is over)! My son and I usually go to the beach once a week on "normal" summers, but this summer has been extremely abnormal with mountains of work from writing this book to recording and singing engagements . . . and on top of that,*

we're doing a little much-needed re-modeling in our home! We do everything ourselves, so therefore it takes up "our" time! It's fun, though, to rip out the 14½-year-old carpet and put down new flooring! Hopefully NASCAR will be doing some "remodeling" projects of their own with next year's Chase format! We'll see . . . But tomorrow, I plan on "parking" my exhausted self down on the beach and enjoying God's wondrous creations . . .
. . . At least for an hour!

The heat is on! On "Fontana Street!"
Beating down unmercifully on every soul in every seat!

The heat's so hot, you feel it deep inside!
You need to drink gallons of Gatorade just to stay alive!

But the real heat lies within that flaming 24-car!
The pressure's on to pad the points on his Bonus-score-card!

Caught up in the action, he could win or lose!
That's the chance you take when the heat's on you!

That flat track is boiling, all greasy and slick!
Stevie Wonder's the Grand Marshall,
The other "Stevie Wonder" leads Team 24 in the pits!

The searing pressure is on Letarte!
I'm sure his blood pressure is up too!
As he ponders and calculates to figure out just what to do!

Jeff's engine is like a pressure cooker,
Trying not to *blow a gasket!*

The team will carefully work together,
Like fragile eggs in one basket!

The crushing burden of the heat,
Adds to the surging challenges that lie ahead!

These guys are tough as nails!
Lesser men would be dead!

Kurt Busch and Jimmie lead this pack of sweaty stars . . .
Jeff rolls off sixteenth, I hope he has a good car!

The pace car pulls off,
The boys drive straight into the sun!
Conditions like this don't make racing very fun!

On the first lap Jeff cruised three positions to thirteenth!
So far it's looking good, looks like that Chevy's full of steam!

Then a tempest breaks out on only lap 8,
Nemecheck's engine gasps for life inside Car 78!

Jeff will pit for four tires, and come out in eighth spot!
Reach for clean air, Jeff, and show us what you've got!

Meanwhile, back on pit road,
"Juan Problem" collides with "Office Depot!"

. . . A quick visit for some supplies?
Somethin' tells me, "I don't think so!"

On lap 12 Jeff and Jr. split Andretti by barely an inch!
. . . John's hungry to rid himself
Of this roasted "Chevy sandwich!"

Gordon was up to fourth,
Then slipped to seventh on lap 22!

Then Sadler spun for a CAUTION,
So Jeff paid a visit to his crew!

Many guys stayed out, so Jeff restarted in twentieth spot!
But by lap 35, he's in ninth, and has moved up a lot!

Mikey's on fire for a CAUTION on lap 39!
He had a left front explosion that cut his oil line!

His 55-car is fried, and from it his large frame emerges!
Jeff makes a quick pit and to ninth spot he surges!

Sauter stayed out to lead but quickly fell back.
Then it's Kyle Busch at the helm leading this feisty pack!

Jeff's in eighth then slips to tenth on lap 57!
Out of nowhere, he's completely sideways!
"No tightness anywhere!" he said!

The track is changing now,
And many cars are going loose!

But Jeff's lap times are still competitive!
No need to whip out the noose!

After a lap 71 CAUTION,
Jr. takes the lead!

I'm sure the announcers are thrilled!
You know they'll surely take heed!

I know Dale's Jeff's future teammate, but give me a break!
If I only had a "buck" tonight for each mention of his name!

. . . They're really wearin' it out!
. . . I'd be a millionaire for sure!

There are other drivers on the track, guys!
Take a break from Jr.'s lure!

What is up with the fixation?! I often wonder to myself!
Give us and Dale a break! Talk about someone else!

There, I've vented! I feel better! It's finally off my chest!
I hope my readers don't mind, but I had no patience left!

I've had it up to the ceiling
With all the "Jr. talk!"

Does anyone else out there feel the need,
About this topic, to squawk?!

Let's head back to the race now, shall we?
It's a CAUTION on lap 111.

Jeff reports that his "buns" feel as hot as . . .
Well——that place opposite of Heaven!

. . . Now that's some kind of HOT!
The ice packs get prepared,
And he moves up to seventh spot!

The 48 of Johnson leads, Jeff's loose, but in sixth,
On lap 125, he moves up to fifth!

Next victim is Burton! He goes by him for fourth!
They keep swapping positions,
Jeff states he's loose in 3 & 4!

He's tight in turns 1 & 2, and has no drive off!
Hang on! Changes are comin', GREEN pits aren't far off!

Steve and the crew keep working on Jeff's car!
Nothing seems to help his horrible conditions thus far!

Then lap 179 turns bad luck to worse!
Jeff slides into Mayfield and multiple cars disperse!

The 24 is slightly damaged, many adjustments are made!
Ricky Rudd's 900th race start ended on a stretcher today!

Much to my ad nauseam,
The DuPont Chevy still has no grip!

But Jeff works his way up all the way
From twenty-third to FIFTH!

When there's a glimmer of hope
For at least a top five finish,

A GREEN pit stop was made,
And his positions *majorly* diminished!

And to make matters worse, he went a lap down!
Has our "mojo" been lost? Has it ditched out of town?

It's after midnight on the east cost
When this nightmare race finally ended!

But all is not lost!
Victory is merely suspended!

A 22nd place finish,
And no bonus points to store,

Will make us hungrier at Richmond
And go after the win once more!

The 48 of Johnson was the victor at this race,
Then The 99, The 5, The 31 then The 8.

11 CAUTIONS in all, and no Bonus points for Jeff!
We might have had a chance had our driver not wrecked!

But after next week,
The BIG Chase will begin!

Time for Jeff to clean up
And go for his 5th Championship win!

We'll follow him closely
Until every last lap!

After he wins next week at Richmond,
There'll be no looking back!

CHAPTER 26

Chevy Rock and Roll 400
Richmond International Raceway

September 8, 2007

*N*othing personal, but Jimmie Johnson is like a bad cough. He just won't go away! As upset as I was at the outcome of this race, at least Jeff had another good finish here! (Although, he should have won! Again!) Can you believe the race results for him and Jimmie were the same as the Richmond race back in May? That's kind of a "freak of nature," don't you think?! Well, next week begins ten weeks of agony as we count down to the Championship! I better run out to the nearest Sam's Club and buy the mother lode supply of anti-acid and Pepto Bismol! My fingernails will not see length again until Christmas! Jeff and Team 24 have been so stellar this year, broken so many records, I just can't imagine him not finishing out this season as our 2007 Champion! He certainly deserves it! Besides that, it would really help the sales of this book if he wouldn't mind winning this year! No, I'm thinking he wouldn't mind at all! So Jeff, see what you can do, will ya, Bro?! Thanks! And so the count-down begins . . . We **know** he can do it! As a matter of fact, we're **sure** of it!

It's just a matter of time . . . !

The saga continues at Richmond this week!
The 26th attempt for illusive bonus points to seek!

Teammates Jimmie and Jeff are ready to *rock and roll!*
Starting first and second, both chase the same goal!

I'm slightly annoyed at this point in my brain,
Jeff was miles ahead in points
Until Jimmie's win upset the game!

So does consistency mean nothing
In this new form of "Chase?"

There's something still a little off
With the logistics of this case!

Put all that aside; all is not lost,
The very end of this season will show Jeff is the BOSS!

No, I'm not prideful,
just an intensely confident fan!

Profoundly hoping and praying
Jeff's championship is part of God's plan!

So the headline tonight is the COT,
Featured on ESPN shown on ABC!

(You either need a high I.Q. or could call the FBI,
To figure out the "P.D.Q.'s" of that one, and that's no lie!)

Jeff jumps up to first, right off the bat!
Jimmie slips back and Gordon leads the first lap!

(Not that the five bonus points
Mean anything at all,

But leading laps is a good thing,
And we want Jeff to lead them all!)

The first CAUTION's out already on just the 8th lap,
The 96 and Jeff Green had some minor contact.

Hamlin's all over Jeff's bumper like grease all over bacon!
Rewind, "Mr. Denny," 'cuz first spot is taken!

But Jeff exits the lead
On a lap 23 CAUTION,

He pits for gas and four tires
And relays his car's pretty awesome!

A few guys stayed out and a couple more took two tires,
Jeff restarts in fifth, and boy, is he on fire!

He passes two right away,
And before you know it, he's vying for first!

Until a CAUTION flag flies on 63,
Shortly after his stop, he resumes first!

Lap 84 shows the fastest in the field is our Jeff!
That's right where we like him—out in front of all the rest!

Jeff's lapping the field, pegging them off one by one,
Until the CAUTION stops the flow on lap 131!

Nemecheck lost a right front,
And Jeff's pit stop was great!

Like a fine-tuned band,
The 24-players are on time, never late!

That 24-team put our Jeff clean out in first place!
Behind him is Edwards, Jimmie Johnson,
Then Hamlin behind The 48.

On 166, The 99 went by Jeff!
The nerve of that *boy* trying to steal his success!

But! As any race fan knows, *anything* can happen!
Carl's engine blew on 182, and he's no longer laughin'!

Jeff will pit on this YELLOW for some much needed "tweaks!"
He's out second behind Hamlin when we go back to GREEN!

Lap 194 shows Jeff
Is just inches from The 11!

They battle hard for position and I yell:
"Come on Jeff, go get him!"

This on-track display of tussle and muscle,
Allowed Bowyer to advance, and now he's in the rustle!

Clint and Denny "go at it,"
Which caused Bowyer to spin!

Jeff repossesses first place
While Stewart takes second from Hamlin!

There's a wreck on 241
And Montoya is on fire!

The 29 and The 2 are panicking!
To finish in the 30's is required!

If Harvick doesn't finish 32nd or better,
Or Busch (who's also damaged), 36th or higher,

Their chance to be in the Chase
Will most likely expire!

Harvick plowed through the grass, now it's stuck in his grill!
Causing a geyser of steam to spray against his will!

(What's the problem, I'm thinking,
Jeff won a race in this form!

Proving those Hendrick engines are stellar
Even when weathered and worn!)

Flames are dominant tonight in more ways than one!
Now Sorensen is on fire right after he spun!

On lap 267, Stewart's too close for my liking!
He goes by Jeff on 270, and my nails I start biting!

Then it gets worse! Jimmie proceeds by Jeff too!
I hope on lap 293's CAUTION Steve will know just what to do!

After pit stops and changes
And a long RED flag for the mess,

Jimmie and Stewart are first and second,
And then the 24-car is next!

"Jimmie and Stewart" aren't making it
A *Wonderful Life* for our guy!

Then the YELLOW's out again,
For the 11th CAUTION of the night!

The 48's out first then it's Jeff then The 8——
The top two positions are exactly how we started this race!

The pressure's on for Dale Jr.,
As we already know!

He has to win and hope he's lucky enough
To make the Chase show!

The next several laps,
Jeff and Jr. fight for position!

Trading spots back and forth
While Jimmie advances to over 3 seconds!

Wouldn't you know it, Jeff wore out his "stuff"!
His tires are now hosed and his car's had enough!

Even the 6-car of Ragan takes third spot from Jeff!
At this local in the race, I'm really losing my head!

There are 10 laps to go and Jeff is in fifth!
This really "bites the wall" for us fans,
And really stinks for him!

Then on 394, for Jr. all hopes were dashed . . .
His engine let go and he smoked off the track.

Jeff moved up to fourth,
And that's where he'll end,

Like the last Richmond race,
When Jimmie also took the win!

Do they sell Nicorette for your ears?
'Cuz there's smoke pouring out of mine!

Jeff should have won this race!
He was incredible all night!

What's happening at these races
At the end where it counts?!

Are we adjusting too much,
For crying out loud?!

"I Can't Smile Without You,"
Has become my weekly theme song . . .

. . . As I sing it to the trophy
Held by hands that are wrong!

O.K., it's time to "buck up!" The pity party is over!
We'll start fresh next week, where Jeff's wins will take over!

New Hampshire awaits "The Best of the Best!"
The 24-team's still got it! We'll prove to the rest!

CHAPTER 27

Sylvania 300
New Hampshire International Speedway

September 16, 2007

And, we're off! So, at the start of this race, Jeff's "hugantuan" points-lead is erased, and he begins in a rare second-place position with 5040 points and Jimmie in first with 5060 points! In case you didn't know, The Chasers all received an even 5000 points plus 10 points for each win they had during the first 26 races of the season. Those win points are the only points that carried over to the start of these last 10 races. Obviously, Jimmie had six wins and Jeff had four. Hence, the points-lead flip! We now just have to pretend that Jeff didn't have an over 300-point lead last week! Such are the rules . . . doesn't mean I have to like them! Tony Stewart is close behind in third with 5030 points, Carl Edwards and Kurt Busch with 5020, and Hamlin, Truex, Kenseth, Kyle Busch, Burton and Harvick all have 5010, and Clint Bowyer rounds off the top 12 with 5000. Wow! That's all very, very close, wouldn't you say?! It doesn't matter, Team 24 can handle it! They have some rules of their own, and that's to win this Championship!

The "Drive for Five" is on! Let's roll!

And so we begin!
It's here in our face!

The last ten races,
And the beginning of The Chase!

And so begins the mass exodus
Of my cerebral cells!

And true test of my neurons
Already completely overwhelmed!

Jeff starts today's crusade in eighteenth position,
With his "bod" fully hydrated and packed full of nutrition!

It's his 500th start! We're so proud of this soul!
He's the youngest active driver to ever reach this goal!

He's got 300 laps to get his points-lead back!
The second we go GREEN he'll begin his attack!

Check out the pole-sitter, I do believe it's Clint!
(That's Bowyer, not Eastwood!) Will it be a brief stint?

Well, the gentlemen started their engines,
They rolled off pit road!
I wonder how many emotions this race will evoke?!

The 24 starts going backwards
At the start of this race!

Low pressures in those Goodyears
Make it tough to keep pace!

Sylvania 300

But by lap 10 he's in eighteenth; back up where he started,
Then from Burton, The 11 and Kyle Busch he departed!

There's a COMPETITION YELLOW on lap 35,
A rain-shortened practice yesterday was the reason why.

Jeff restarts in twelfth and Bowyer still leads . . .
. . . What in the world did Clint do
To obtain that kind of speed?!

By lap 50, Jeff's "on it" and really checking them off!
He's in ninth, moving forward while the other guys scoff!

Next it's Earnhardt then Newman,
And then a CAUTION ensues!

Jeff's out behind Stewart
In position number two!

He battles with Tony, really trying to get by!
Just a tad bit more; he's only four-tenths behind!

While they fight for position, Bowyer sneaks up behind Jeff!
Then goes by him on 81!
——Jeff says he's loose, but I'll bet he's tense!

Kurt Busch lost a cylinder on lap 122;
Not a healthy thing for a "Chaser,"
——Which most likely ruined his mood!

GREEN-flag pits began around lap 133——
Right after Harvick had issues——looks like a flat tire to me!

Jeff moved up to second shortly after his stop!
"Come on, let's boogie!" "We've got a field to mop!"

Gordon will pit for "right sides" at the CAUTION on 164,
And you know what they say, "Cautions only breed more!"

. . . There's another on 169 when Schrader and The 41 spin!
Harvick barely skims by, narrowly missing them!

Then again on 180,
Earnhardt "twirls" by himself . . .

Looking like a music video
For that old-fashioned tune "Twist and Shout!"

You won't believe it! Another CAUTION! (See what I mean?!)
On lap 187, into Blaney, Regan screams!

Jeff and Tony Stewart are at it again,
They both want fourth spot, but Jeff ends up in fifth!

Then my angst takes a U-turn around lap 220 or so,
When Jeff smokes right by Stewart for third place in the row!

Kyle Busch is in second, but soon Jeff had that spot!
It was The 5's turn to pit! Thanks, Kyle, a lot!

Jeff continues to dig hard,
To go after Clint!

While Bowyer pinches himself
Because of the position he's in!

He's been in front most all day, and may get his first win!
Unfortunately for us Gordon fans, his engine just won't quit!

Jeff's in heavy lap traffic, but still in second place!
Does any hope remain with eight laps left in this race?

Sylvania 300

All of a sudden, Clint Bowyer states
That he feels a vibration!

Will his first win be dashed
In front of this great NASCAR Nation?

Well, no such luck for us Gordon fans,
But what fantastic team skill!
Getting Jeff from eighteenth to second with power and will!

Jeff's got his points-lead back,
Although with teammate, Jimmie, he's tied!

Sorry, Jimmie, you'll have to go,
First place isn't built for two-wide!

Jeff will resume his throne next week
With a performance extraordinaire!
With fever and drive up in Dover, Delaware!

The home of DuPont!
His great sponsor in the north!

A win for them would be awesome,
And for us fans too, of course!

But this week it's Bowyer's first win in 64 starts.
And his boss is in Mongolia, hunting? **Oh my stars!**

Are there not enough animals
In the "U.S. of A?"

Man, he should have seen the jungle
On the New Hampshire track here today!

Stewart, Kyle and Truex round out the top five.
Then it's Jimmie, then Kenseth, then Car 25.

The points shuffled madly after this first race of The Chase!
The drama will continue at the very next race!

So "buckle up" and take notice,
Only nine more to go!

'Till our "Champ" takes his 5th Cup!
I just feel it in my bones!!

CHAPTER 28

Dodge Dealers 400
Dover International Speedway

September 23, 2007

*I'd like to wish my nephew, Stephen, a Happy Birthday, today! He is **24**! A most excellent number! ☺ Happy **24**th, "Estefan!" As for today's race, two words: "Monster Mile." Nuff said. Read on . . .*
You, too, will believe in monsters!

We return with trepidation to this "barbaric beast,"
Known by most as the "Monster Mile!"

You'll see what I mean, observe for yourself,
If you "hang" with me at Dover for a while!

To make matters worse, Jimmie Johnson starts first,
And Jeff's "clogged" back in TWENTY-SEVENTH!

This Chase removes weekly, years from my life,
I feel soon I could "meet my Maker" up in Heaven!

We've got 400 laps—that's 400 miles!
Of concrete and COT giving us grief!

The last time we were here, Jeff's car was looser than loose,
And nothing really gave him relief!

But Jeff's got the most wins here,
More than any active driver . . .
. . . Haven't I mentioned this statement before?!

You know he and the crew will give it their all,
And try and add to the win list, one more!

Between laps 1 and 2, Hamlin gets Jimmie loose,
And leads, though Denny's sick as a dog!

Right away we notice that ole' 24-car,
Begins to dislocate himself from that clog!

He activates some action, for a great chain reaction,
Of grinding off positions one by one!

By just lap 11, he's up to eighteenth!
Watching your driver advance is what makes racing fun!

Uh oh, here we go; the first CAUTION is thrown!
Sauter and The 38 clash in turn 4.

Another CAUTION on lap 20, but Jeff keeps moving forward!
On lap 43 he's up to tenth on the board!

By only lap 45, Jeff's advanced nineteen spots!
But the announcers are talking so much about Jr.,
They don't notice!

Dodge Dealers 400

Hello! There are "Chasers" on the track,
If you could focus on them,
To us listeners it would be a real bonus!

Then all starts to wane as we hear our Jeff say,
"I'm starting to lose the drive-off," on lap 66!

A few laps later, the YELLOW flag waves,
A prime opportunity to get that DuPont Impala fixed!

All turns a little scary in The 55's pit,
When the gasman, Art Harris, by a bouncing tire was hit!

The hospital reported later that he was awake and alert!
We certainly wish him well and hope he's not badly hurt!

We go back to GREEN on lap 84,
With the 2-car of Kurt Busch in the lead.

Next it's Biffle then Mears and then Carl Edwards,
In fifth spot is Car 17.

Sixth place is Hamlin, seventh, *our Jeff*,
Then it's Kyle Busch who seals the top eight.

Then for some strange reason, Jeff starts to go backwards,
This happens on lap 88!

On 91 he's in tenth, 103 in eleventh, 122 in twelfth . . .
And so continues his fate!

He's unbearably loose and barely holding on!
We need a Caution before it's too late!

My wish came true on 147,
With a CAUTION to let Harris' ambulance out.

Two rounds in the left rear, two rubbers and wedge,
Are the instructions Steve Letarte called out!

Even after those adjustments, he's still way loose!
What is up with that car and this track?!

If the thing would run right at this unforgiving place,
I swear, I wouldn't know how to act!

But some of the other Chase drivers are way worse off . . .
. . . Like Harvick for instance, exits singing a sad song . . . !

"You picked a fine time to leave me "loose wheel!"
. . . Not his anthem of choice, yes, for Kevin it's just wrong!

Next Jimmie cut a tire and Stewart went a lap down!
I guess Jeff in eleventh isn't the worst car in town!

The trouble continues for more Chasers you see,
Burton goes a lap down and Hamlin crashes Kyle Petty!

This brings out a CAUTION on lap 204,
Jeff will pull into the pits
To work on that heinous car some more!

He's out in ninth place, which isn't too bad!
Then three guys go by him, which makes *Maria* really mad!

You'll never believe who's now battling Jeff for position!
In my disbelief and horror, It's Mikey Waltrip on a mission!

Dodge Dealers 400

Waltrip *passes* Jeff on lap 227!
Surely you jest! This has happened almost never!

Another CAUTION, more adjustments on 228,
The 17's running well and continues to dominate!

I can't believe my ears,
Now Jeff is *too tight?!*

Can someone find the secret
To getting these adjustments exactly right?!

Perhaps Carl Edwards knows; he just passed Kenseth for first!
Then on 278 for Jeff, we go from bad to worse!

He's in sixteenth position,
And there's only seventeen on the lead lap!

Mark Martin, the leader,
Is hot on his back!

Sure enough, he goes down, on lap 309,
Until he gets his lap back when Martin pits out of sight!

Lap 313 shows Jeff in sixth,
The highest he's been all day!

. . . But don't get too excited,
In this positive position, he won't stay!

It's time for more adjustments
By "Dr. Steve" and his team,

They work hard for a diagnosis,
But that Chevy's plagued with a mystery disease!

Jeff's now 1½ laps down in sixteenth position!
Time to pray for a miracle, good luck or attrition!

Kenseth is down a cylinder
And Edwards takes over first.

With only six cars on the lead lap,
This "Monster Mile" must be cursed!

Between lap 354 and 380,
There's four CAUTION'S and a RED FLAG!

Matt Kenseth lost an engine
in the midst of that fray!

Then on lap 386, there's a honkin' big wreck!
Claiming twelve cars, and once again we *see RED!*

We return to GREEN on 390,
And Jeff's in thirteenth!

Ten laps to try for a top-ten
And pretend we've got some speed!

Well this race is FINALLY over!
What a long day!

It felt longer than the Coke 600!
Seems like we really wore out our stay!

Now that all the pain and suffering is over,
It really didn't turn out too bad!

Jeff ended up eleventh,
But FIRST in points, WOO HOO!
In case you happen to be keeping tabs!

"Concrete Carl" was first
And obviously solid as a rock!

Somehow he beat "The Monster"
And was fastest on the block!

The points shuffle again, like we knew they would do.
You can see for yourself, I'll post them for you:

1st	Jeff Gordon!	
2nd	Tony Stewart	-2
3rd	Carl Edwards	-3
4th	Jimmie Johnson	-4
5th	Kyle Busch	-10
6th	Clint Bowyer	-18
7th	Martin Truex	-46
8th	Jeff Burton	-75
9th	Kevin Harvick	-115
10th	Matt Kenseth	-116
11th	Kurt Busch	-151
12th	Denny Hamlin	-158

Now Dover's behind us!
We can be thankful for that!

Now we'll focus on Kansas
And the success there we've had!

The wisdom of the Scarecrow, to Steve we bequeath!
Strength and courage of the Lion in Jeff, you know we'll see!

The team will work like the Tin Man,
With every ounce of heart!

We'll click our heals together
And off to Victory Lane we'll depart!

"There's no place like home in Victory Lane,"
I always say!

Don't you know this crazy season's left me singing,
"If I only had a brain?!"

But prepare yourself,
Aunt Em, Dorothy and Toto too!

To Kansas Speedway a geostrophic tornado with flames
Is about to blow through!

CHAPTER 29

LifeLock 400
Kansas Speedway

September 30, 2007

*This chapter of my book I would humbly like to dedicate to my
dear brother-in-law and Tony Stewart fan, Jeff Eldred!
With Love, Your Favorite Sister-In-Law, Maria
P.S. Always remember:
It aint over, 'TIL IT'S OVER! ☺*

From Dover to Mid-America,
We find the third race of this Chase!

Today's outlandish plot will either make you a "believer,"
Or in a big way shake your faith!

The crazy events, twists and turns
Would cause even the Wizard of Oz to scratch his head!

The saga that continues
In the Chase for the Cup,

Could cause even the Wicked Witch of the West
To rise from the dead!

"Resting on our laurels" is never an option,
Until the day this Chase is won!

Grabbing every point and position we can,
Striving never to be part of that "Big One!"

There's a fierce wind at Kansas Speedway today,
Similar to the one that ushered Dorothy to Oz!

You won't believe how the winds of change will blow,
And how Jeff astonishingly beat negative odds!

Jeff qualified fourth, with Jimmie on the pole,
This in-house rivalry refuses to end!

But Jimmie started in the rear because in the final practice,
His primary car had a wreck!

But like in any crazy "soap opera" or movie of choice,
Some *strange twists of events* must take place!

There was a shuffle in the points, just since last week,
Even before the GREEN flew for this race!

You see, Mr. Carl Edwards, our winner last week,
Came up short upon post-race inspection!

He was docked 25 points, and the result was a move
From third in points to a sixth-place deflection!

So, back to today.
Time to get this re-cap under way . . .

LifeLock 400

Jeff's hot on Kenseth's tail,
Right after the GREEN flag waved!

They run one and two,
But just for the first few,

'Cuz on lap 11 is the CAUTION,
And then the RED flag flew too!

Rain was the culprit that brought a halt to this race!
When we were just getting going, and picking up pace!

But the rain soon ceased
And the track dried up quick,

Thanks to the dryers and the wind
That just gusted and whipped!

Jeff came in for four tires; others took two,
He restarts eleventh and is in hot pursuit!

Jeff Burton was sent to the tail end of the line,
He touched his car under RED, and now he was fined!

The 24's up to eighth by lap 26,
Then two laps later there's a CAUTION 'cuz the 5-car was hit!

Jr. rear-ended Kyle and put him into the wall,
Accepting full responsibility and admitting his fault!

Jeff restarted in fourth, and by lap 32 is in third!
Another CAUTION on 33? This is getting absurd!

Truex cut his right-front and slammed into the wall!
Upon another one of the "Chasers," this bad luck did fall!

Matt Kenseth is the leader, then The 2 and then Jeff,
Until Kurt goes by Matt, and with him Jeff on the left!

A quick YELLOW on lap 60,
Jeff's in for four tires and out FIRST!

Jeff's hungry for top position,
But overcome by Matt's *thirst!*

Who's that behind Jeff? Please tell me it's a lie!
The 20 of Stewart, that ole' thorn in my side!

Tony swipes first on lap 74!
On lap 75, Jeff's real tight and in fourth!

Now we start the same pattern
That's been from one week to the next——

We start out good and strong,
Then soon after we're hexed!

Jeff continues to fall backwards,
Is even passed by The 48!

We need Glinda's magic wand,
But it appears she's running late!

Lap 118 Jeff's seventh,
But rapidly begins his downward decent!

By 135 he's pushing like a dump truck,
And is slipping out of tenth!

On lap 140 GREEN flag pit stops start,
Which always makes me nervous!

LifeLock 400

If a CAUTION came out, after Jeff stops,
It would do him a great disservice!

Well, what'd'ya know, much to my horror,
A CAUTION flag was thrown!

Jeff's caught a lap down in 30th position,
While Stewart leads the show!

Tony's about out of gas, but he stays out anyway,
Due to lightning and rain on the horizon!

Hoping the race will be called instead of just RED-flagged,
And to Victory Lane he could drive in!

If the race stops here, Jeff would be caught in the rear,
In the race but more importantly in the standings!

Tensions are high, as buckets drop from the sky,
There's a monsoon today in Kansas!

Most assume the race is over,
And Tony Stewart has won!

They see a saturating deluge
And no chance for the sun!

Even some of the drivers
Took a shower and changed!

They thought anyone hoping for more racing today
Was surely deranged!

But I never gave up!
I never heard the "fat lady" sing!

I prayed for a miracle,
And from my own "pipes" let it ring . . .

"SOMEWHERE, over the rainbow,
Skies are blue!"

And the dreams that I'm daring to dream,
In a couple of hours **really might come true!**

And sure enough, that mock hurricane
Finally disappeared!

We're going back to GREEN,
And there's hope for all my fears!!!

I wished upon a star and prayed to my God,
And woke up where the clouds were far behind me!

My troubles melted like lemon drops!
Away above the flag-stand tops!
Flying high you'll find me!

There's a chance, there's a hope, to dig out of this trench!
The 24-team is ready! No more sitting on "the bench!"

Their work clothes are on! Their gloves are pulled tight!
They're ready with their driver to advance with a fight!

On 155, we're finally underway!
The long wait is over! Time to return to the race!

But as quickly as it starts, we stop, **yet again!**
There's a multi-car wreck with numerous cars in the fence!

Jeff skims through by the skin of his teeth!
The carnage-filled mess goes seven cars deep!

Stewart got a piece, but refuses to pit!
It's because of this decision he'll take a points hit!

Jeff pits twice for some "tweaks"
And to top off with gas,

That will hopefully move him forward,
Though now he's close to last!

We go back to GREEN
And Stewart's smokin' like crazy!

He's having trouble controlling his "wagon"
But is showing he's not lazy!

He falls to eighteenth while Jeff moves toward the front!
Harvick and Biffle switch around for a turn in position one!

On lap 174,
Jeff passed Tony for eighteenth!

But the next lap is what does it,
And has Stewart really steamed!

The 2 ran into The 20,
and The 20 into The 99!

"You **ARE** the weakest link, Tony!"
To you we wave, **"GOOD BYE !"**

Another CAUTION right after this last one——
Can't these boys drive nice?

Haven't we had enough mishaps?
Do we really need this much "spice?!"

Denny Hamlin and McMurray
Brought this last Caution out,

Then Denny was BLACK-flagged
'Cuz he was dragging something around!

There are * **24** * laps left
When we go back to GREEN.

Watch out, boys, Jeff's got new tires,
Right along with a full head of steam!

On 188, he's 16th!
13th on 189!

. . . And you know what I always say:

"If happy little bluebirds fly, then why, oh why, can't I?!"

He does fly! On 190, he's taken over twelfth!
On 191 he's eleventh! ***That's what I'm talkin' about!***

193, he's in tenth, and then quickly to ninth!
If only, **IF ONLY**, we had a little more daylight!

Lap 195 he's to seventh, then quickly he takes sixth!
By lap 200, he's in the top five, positioned up in fifth!

There's a CAUTION (doggone it!) on lap 206.
Juan "Problem" Montoya had a tire that split!

Then NASCAR called the race!
It's just too dark to take risks!

I bet Jeff would have won,
If that track were just lit!

Biffle takes the checkers.
(Though he never really made it that far!)

More confusion and controversy . . .
Ya gotta love NASCAR!

Bowyer was second,
Then The 48.

Casey Mears and then Jeff!
What incredible fate!

Jeff's now second in the standings,
Just 6 points behind The 48!

But it could have been worse
Had the rain kept on and dried a little too late!

At one juncture this day,
To the Scarecrow I could relate!

I felt like my stuffing was ripped out
And someone else had my brain!

But just as Dorothy, her friends, and yes, Toto, too!
Kept to their journey, though hardships ensued!

That great 24-team with a Champion Wizard named Jeff,
Kept slugging along, until they had nothing left!

Kansas City turned Emerald,
With a great top five finish!

Now we'll drive off to Talladega,
Where there, **WE WILL WIN IT!**

CHAPTER 30

UAW-Ford 500
Talladega Superspeedway

October 7, 2007

*W*ell, today is the introduction of the new COT car to the superspeedway! With all of the "unknowns" of how this car would handle going 200 mph all day, and with the history of the "Big One" that usually always occurs at this track, Jeff decided to play it safe and hang out in the back for the majority of the afternoon and try and avoid any unnecessary mishaps! **We don't need any mishaps!** The race was a little on the boring side, **until the very end, that is!** Then it was all worth the wait! What an incredible finish! Today was truly a re-enforcement of the statement:
"Good things come to those who wait!"

Well, it doesn't look like we're in Kansas anymore!
We are definitely at Talladega and ready to roar!!

It's Waltrip on the pole, a "freak of nature" in itself!
Way do go, Mikey, you Qualifying stealth!

What about our Jeff? Is that him in **36th?**
Don't worry about it, folks, this is a problem he can fix!

It's all part of the plan he and Steve have cooked up!
To come from "deep weeds" all the way to the front!

It's the COT's first introduction to a Superspeedway thus far!
Five hundred miles of unknowns with this "beast" of a car!

Tug those belts tightly; don't go below the yellow line!
Keep cool under pressure, and *hopefully* all will be fine!

The unknowns are "weirding" me out!
I'm feeling light in the head!

The race hasn't even started,
And I'm already half-dead!

"Get a handle on your sanity!"
I say to myself!

"A mind is a terrible thing to waste,
And losing yours won't help!"

I watch that white-flamed, Pepsi car
Move forward at the GREEN!

That is one cool, hot car,
With that Pepsi flame-scheme!

Blaney led the first lap,
Mikey couldn't hold him off.

We'll see if he can re-gain that speed
That he's temporarily lost!

208

UAW-Ford 500

CAUTION's out on lap 17;
A cut tire for The 49.

Hamlin leads at the GREEN,
While Jeff and Jimmie hang around 39th!

On lap 31, Jr.'s "nation" wigged out!
There was an abnormal departure
Of shrieks, shrills and shouts!

The 8 was in the lead,
And the whole world knew it!

The ESPN guy "guaranteed" he'd win today,
But with that statement, *I guarantee* HE BLEW IT!

Another YELLOW came out on lap 63,
For Gilliland and Biffle——

Do you suppose each other
They couldn't see?

Hamlin's still the leader,
And all remains about the same . . .

Jeff's hanging out in the back
Waiting for this lack of excitement to change!

Personally, I'm a little lethargic,
And could use a *Starbucks Double Shot!*

This tenseness is overbearing,
But real exciting, it's really not!

A single file line with Hamlin in the lead,
And Jeff at the tail end, holding back on his speed!

Lap 83 shows Nemecheck
Spittin' fluid and smokin'!

He was BLACK-flagged by NASCAR,
And you know they weren't jokin'!

. . . I'm a little concerned (As if I need any more stress!)
It's an HMS engine! Now there's apprehension for the rest!

The explosions continue when The 31 blew!
This "Chaser" lost his engine on lap 92!

We're led to the GREEN again,
By Car 55!

He's happy to prove to his sponsors
That he really does know how to drive!

Another "Chaser's" engine
Came un-glued on 113!

Coming from the car and Truex's ears
Was a full head of steam!

Jeff's still in the back with 55 laps to go!
He can't wait for the signal to "Get up and GO!"

Speaking of "get up and go," Jr.'s car "Got up and went!"
On lap 136, his motor was spent!

His "guaranteed win"
Won't happen today!

UAW-Ford 500

"Someone's" eating the words they spoke
At the start of this race!

Things got a little crazy
When Jeff went in to pit!

The air wrench hose got hung in his car,
Then thrown from his pit!

NASCAR issued Jeff a Stop-and-Go PENALTY,
And BOY, WAS HE MAD!!!

But could this be a plan
From our "Heavenly Dad?"

God works in mysterious ways,
And what looked like his demise,
Turned out to become a total blessing in disguise!

He was far away from the BIG ONE that happened on 144!
Which collected Kyle and Kenseth, The 11 and more!

Now it's time to "get the lead out"
And Jeff restarts in eighteenth!

Ready to make a tear,
You just wait and see!

Jeff's seventeenth on lap 150, then **ninth on 152!**
We're cruisin' now, people, and in wicked hot pursuit!

The seventh CAUTION breaks the momentum on 153,
Schrader had the issue and Stewart took the lead!

Another YELLOW shortly after!
Kyle Petty's hard in the wall!

Then the slicing and dicing resumed
When the GREEN flag took its fall!

Jeff's in ninth on the outside,
The inside lane is bearing down fast!

Jeff wanted to drop down,
But that lane was a hypersonic blast!

Now he's back in thirteenth, but one lap later, in tenth!
Another CAUTION on 175 leaves a slight on-track mess!

There'll be an 8-lap shoot out when we go back to GREEN!
Stewart's dying to win here and is desperate for the lead!

Lap 180, Jeff's in seventh!
181, he's in sixth!

182, in the top five,
Then immediately to third on the list!

There's deafening screams
From our family room today!

As he moves to second behind Jimmie;
And Mears behind **him** in the relay!

The 20's coming quickly, hard on the outside,
When Casey moves to the center groove!

Dave Blaney bumps Jeff in the rear,
And The 24 makes his move!

UAW-Ford 500

He jumps out in front of The 20,
Like the "super hero" he is!

Then Stewart slammed him in front of Jimmie,
And in the nick of time, HE WINS!!!!!!!!

I quickly check my pulse to see if I'm still alive!
I know one thing that's alive, and that's the "Drive for Five!"

It's the 2007
Talladega sweep!

His twelfth superspeedway victory
Makes this guy unique!

His methodical patience
Truly paid off!

For this 80th career win!
(Sure glad I don't play Sunday golf!)

The team drenches him in Pepsi!
Kudos to Steve and the crew!

Making all the right moves,
And knowing just what to do!

What a celebration!
Ella's first trip to Victory Lane!

——She wants everyone to know that her arrival
Didn't slow her daddy down in *ANY* way!

She has a puzzled look
On her precious, humble face!

But she'll get used to these celebrations;
They'll become a common place!

No place better for a Gordon family portrait,
Than smack in the middle of Victory Lane!

I say we repeat it next week in Charlotte,
The Hendrick Motorsports' State!

Here are the points as we stand:
(Notice Jeff's at the TOP!)

Six Chase-races left!
(No plans for that 24-Team to stop!)

1.	JEFF GORDON !	
2.	Jimmie Johnson	- 9
3.	Clint Bowyer	- 63
4.	Tony Stewart	- 154
5.	Kevin Harvick	- 202
6.	Carl Edwards	- 205
7.	Kurt Busch	- 215
8.	Kyle Busch	- 260
9.	Denny Hamlin	- 262
10.	Martin Truex, Jr.	- 300
11.	Matt Kenseth	- 318
12.	Jeff Burton	- 336

CHAPTER 31

Bank of America 500
Lowe's Motor Speedway

October 13, 2007

*Today is the wedding of someone **extremely special** to me. The wedding is at 4:00pm, and the race coverage begins at 7:00pm, actual race not until around 8:00pm. You do the math. Should be enough time, right? Wow, was I off! Anyone else, and my R.S.V.P. would have been "cannot attend." But this gal is like a daughter to me. The only way I would miss her wedding is for my own funeral! You see, several years ago, her mom and I were both dying of severe illnesses at the same time. Her mom went on to be with the Lord, and I am still here. From that point on, I took it upon myself to take her under my wing, and "mother" her all I could. She had just turned 14 when her mom passed away, and it just broke my heart. A young, teenage girl without a mom. I can't imagine . . . So, anyway, you can see why I had to go to this wedding! The wedding was at a gorgeous church down in Palm Beach, and the reception was at the Flagler Museum! Hello! We're not talking about a bowl of nuts and finger sandwiches here! It's not like I could escape the reception before the meal was served! Hors d'oeuvre's were from 6:00pm to 7:00pm (which I did not know about in advance). I was sweating*

*bullets the whole time! It was now after 8:00pm and we were just being served a most incredible meal! I know her dad must have spent a fortune for this most decadent reception, and there was no way I could be rude and just leave! I was having a friend of mine record the race, so at least I knew I could go back and watch the beginning. I was still antsy. I **needed** to be watching the race! I felt like some sort of drug addict going through withdrawals or something! I also had my portable T.V. in the car and watched as much as I could on the way home! And take notes, in the dark! (How bad have I got it?!) I think we arrived home around 9:30pm and all was well with the world! The race lasted until after midnight, so I got a good "chunk" of it in! I did go back and watch what my friend had taped for me! I have never heard so much overboard talk about Dale Jr. in all of my born days!! I mean, it was just pathetic! I have absolutely nothing against Dale Jr., and don't hold it against him at all. Poor guy, he can't help what his name is! Anyway, I got my point across in this re-cap, so I'll not elaborate! Thank you, in advance for letting me vent! And what an incredible night for Jeff as well!*
"Icing on the 'wedding' cake!"

There's an "Outlandish Ogre,"
Just waiting to pounce!

On any of the "Chasers,"
Their points position to renounce!

"He" waits in turn 4
With a glare that won't cease!

Ready for any takers,
It's the "Beast of the Southeast!"

The NASCAR boys are at home,
Here in Charlotte, North Carolina!

216

Yes, you know they're tough as nails,
But also more fragile than China!

It's a 1 ½ mile risk,
At least 333 times!

With this smooth, slippery track,
And turn 4's evil eyes!

They don't call Lowe's Motor Speedway
A "Beast" for no reason!

It's here you prove your skill,
Or completely louse up your season!

"Flyin' Ryan" is on the pole,
Leading this scary parade,

While Jeff holds down the fort,
Three behind in fourth place!

The Grand Marshall rocked the crowd
With her incredible call!

I can see why she won the contest!
Johnny Fink out-yelled them all!

Well, just after take-off,
And Ryan starts flyin',

The YELLOW waved in lap 1!
Of this I'm not lyin'!

The "Beast" is hungry tonight!
Reutimann receives the first bite!

How many more will be "chewed up,"
And spit out here this night?

Jeff's back to sixth by lap number 10;
The 26-car leads Johnson, Ryan Newman and the rest!

By lap 21, it's the next CAUTION of the night!
David Ragan pinched the wall and quickly found his plight!

Jeff's out nineteenth while Robby Gordon leads——
An interesting switch to what we normally see!

The 29th lap, finds The 29's tires,
Heading down pit road, he thought his right-sides expired!

But by lap 42, he discovered a glitch!
It wasn't the right-sides, but the left's giving fits!

The assessment on 29
Was a misdiagnosis!

As bad as thinking your breath is fresh,
When you've got severe halitosis!

Now he's 3 ugly laps down,
And his "fun" night is *toast!*

It won't be a win this week
That'll give him reason to boast!

Jimmie re-gains the lead on lap 47.
On 65 there's an issue with car number "one seven!"

Matt thinks he's blowing up,
Or his alternator is fried!

But switching batteries
Seems to be a temporary fix for this guy!

There are two more CAUTIONS—
That ole' "Beast" struck again!

Jeff's in eighth behind Jr.,
And "taps" his rear-end!

You would have thought the world ended,
And he didn't even spin!

Jr. lost a few spots,
But it's a race that we're in!

How many times in history
Has Jr. done this same move?!

I thought Rusty Wallace
was going to come completely un-glued!

Accusing Jeff of "peddling"
Just as hard as he can,

To get away from Jr.? Yeah, right!
Jeff's no scaredy cat!

The fuss that was made over poor Number 8,
Would make a grown adult toss the cuisine he just ate!

There's no place for bias
If you're a "professional" commentator!

Time to exit the "booth"
And become a spectator!

I could go on for hours on this very topic!
But to protect my reputation, now's a good time to stop it!

Kenseth's hard in the wall
For the seventh CAUTION of the night!

The poor guy can't buy a break,
He probably wants to give up the fight!

By 161, Bowyer leads and Jeff's in twelfth.
But he's moving forward quickly like a jet-engined stealth!

CAUTION again,
On lap 175!

Sadler's in the wall,
And Jeff states that in the middle he's tight!

The 20's pit stop was truly *the pits* for him!
Contact with The 9, he sent Kasey for a spin!

Clint Bowyer's the leader right out of the pits,
Then it's Kyle, McMurray, Jimmie and Jeff in fifth and sixth!

The 48 seized the lead on lap 185.
On 187, Jeff's up to third in the line!

After CAUTION 10 on lap 206,
Jeff's out in first place, the spot we take comfort in!

Then what to my wondering eyes did appear?
On lap 230, Jimmie spinning?
But this is "his house," so I hear!

The eviction notice has been posted!
It's not your house any more!

Your "room's" been rented out
By Car 24!

With five consecutive DNF's
Since 2004,

This unfriendly neighborhood
Will welcome Jeff Gordon once more!

But he'll have to first "earn his keep"
And it's going to be tough!

The clientele in this area
Is pretty darn rough!

He'll have to clean up this "hood,"
Where his win's been stolen five times!

He'll have to weed out the "riff raff"
One at a time!

He begins with Scott Riggs on lap 244!
He's now in third place, and hunts down some more!

Next it's Newman for second,
He won't be bullied this time!

He won't take any junk from Bowyer,
And is thinking, "the 07 is mine!"

Sure enough he claims first spot,
On lap 272!

Then a cylinder was lost
On car number 2!

Another "Chaser" in trouble;
Is Jeff's luck running thin?

With the year that he's had,
I don't think so, Tim!

Yet another CAUTION on lap 279!
Juan Montoya and Riggs have a turn-two collide!

Jeff pits for adjustments and comes out second behind Kyle,
But soon after re-claims HIS position, Jeff Gordon style!

With 35 laps to go, we all hold our breath!
Praying for at least 500 miles, and not a lap less!

Jeff's got a four-second lead
And requests silence 'til 10 to go!

With unflinching determination
Not to "stink up" his show!

With 23 laps to the finish, Jimmie's up to eighth place!
If we could only stay GREEN until the end of this race!

Then just what we didn't need,
A CAUTION then a RED with 12 to go!

What could possibly happen now?
Nobody really knows!

The "gangs" of "thieves" are back together,
Just ready to attack!

Just when the "Welcome Wagon" for Jeff,
Even dared to come back!

We restart on 329, and Newman passed by Jeff!
Jeff assumed he was out of gas with only one lap left!

As Newman pulls away,
And my heart sinks to my toes,

The 12 spins and is out of Jeff's way!
Woo Hoo! There he goes!

Now we have a GREEN/WHITE checker!
But will Jeff have enough gas?!

This is pure "Midnight Madness!"
My heart beats immeasurably fast!

Bowyer shot him in the bumper
And his restart was great!

He's pulling away fast,
And from the coalition escapes!

Hold on tightly, Jeff! Keep hard on the gas!
That DNF monkey is slipping off your back!

JEFF CROSSED THE FINISH LINE FIRST!
HE WINS AT LMS!!!!

AND FOR AN INCREDIBLE BURN OUT,
HE HAS ENOUGH *PETROL* LEFT!

Call the Home-owners Association!
There's a new resident at "this house!"

It appears that Mr. Johnson, for the time being,
Has moved out!

Clint Bowyer finishes second
Then Kyle, Burton, and Edwards.

Jimmie Johnson's in fourteenth,
And owns a new "out of town" address!

Next week we're headed to Martinsville
Where Jeff is rarely beat!

Can we pull off 3 in a row?
Well now, we'll just have to see!

Jeff's FIRST in the standings,
Again, I'll list them for you...

There's no stopping this driver
And his "Drive for Five" crew!

1.	Jeff Gordon	5880	Leader
2.	Jimmie Johnson	5812	-68
3.	Clint Bowyer	5802	-78
4.	Tony Stewart	5682	-198
5.	Carl Edwards	5640	-240
6.	Kyle Busch	5600	-280
7.	Kurt Busch	5565	-315
8.	Kevin Harvick	5552	-328
9.	Denny Hamlin	5531	-349
10.	Jeff Burton	5514	-366
11.	Martin Truex Jr.	5502	-378
12.	Matt Kenseth	5438	-442

CHAPTER 32

Subway 500
Martinsville Speedway

October 21, 2007

*Y*ou may have heard the saying: "If you want a rainbow, you have to put up with the rain." Well, right now, Jimmie Johnson is the perfect storm! The only reason I can put up with him winning, **again**, is because I know our "Rainbow Warrior" will prevail by the end of this Chase! (At least I hope I know!) But I have to say—all this "thunder and lightning" is making it difficult to sleep at night! AND, the nightmares aren't too pleasant either! But, despite The 48's "continual dropping," the sun is still shining at Martinsville today, (here in Florida, too, by the way!) and we WILL survive the fact that Jeff didn't win today, at "his" track! AND, we'll just try to ignore the fact that he had the pole and led the most laps! **We won't let those things bother us at all, now, will we?!** No! Of course not! Right? Right! ⸺ I know I must be losing it, because I am talking to myself and answering my own questions, but the scariest thing is that **my imaginary friend just told me I have serious problems!** If I didn't know of other NASCAR fans that go through this same type of hysteria, I would go make my reservations at the nearest "resort asylum" right now! **BUT**, what if my "new home" didn't have a television

or any way to tune in to the race next week?! Or what if they only had **one** *T.V. and I had to fight off some "crazy person" who would rather watch re-runs of Charlie Brown's The Great Pumpkin?!*
Then, I would really go nuts!

"Blue skies, smiling at me!"
"Nothing but blue skies do I see!"

With the sun shining brightly
On Martinsville's historic face,

And Jeff on the pole,
Our Ace sets the pace!

It's his seventh pole this season of 2007!
It's no wonder to the Championship this driver is headin'!

He must be cautious today!
Try not to lose his cool or his brakes!

Keep those points up,
'Cuz there's so much at stake!

He's a seven-time winner at this paperclip-shaped track!
He doesn't need coaching! He knows how to act!

The Heritage of America Band plays our National Anthem!
T 38 C Talons buzz the arousing on-track action!

70,000 on their feet! A "bazillion" more at home!
Wait with trepidation for the GREEN flag to be thrown!

I seem to be out of my mind!
I'll be back when the race is over!

Subway 500

I wish a guaranteed great finish
Was simple as gripping a four-leaf clover!

This 10-week Chase action will fry your nerves
If given half the chance!

Will our guy keep his points lead
And never look back?!

Well, "back the truck up,"
Let's take one lap at a time!

If you look too far ahead,
You'll freak out in no time!

We start off this race,
Looking pretty daggone good!

Jeff led the 1st lap
Like we knew that he would!

We'll take those five points,
And any more we can add!

By lap 24,
It's the field he's about to lap!

Ten cars have been put down, by lap 42,
So far that DuPont Chevy is driving nice and smooth!

Lap 44 displays a CAUTION!
The 7's right front tire fried!

Straight into the wall,
His car did collide!

Jeff pits for four tires,
He's first out of the gate!

Behind him is Harvick,
And then, Oh no! The 48!

By lap 62, Jimmie's by Harvick for second place!
That's a little too close for comfort!
Can't Jimmie slow up his pace?!

Like that Martinsville locomotive just past the back straight,
There's an HMS procession on lap 78!

First it's Jeff and next Jimmie, then Kyle in third!
Then it's trouble on lap 80 for a CAUTION, so I heard!

Harvick and Kyle almost *bit the dust!*
Harvick "threaded the needle,"
And found his spotter he can trust!

Another CAUTION waved on lap 92!
Those spotters earned their paychecks today,
Right along with every crew!

Jeff's "loose in and loose off" on lap 109!
Jimmie steals the opportunity and unfortunately goes by!

There's a CAUTION on 112,
And The 01 doesn't look good!

It appears there's a bonfire blazing
Just underneath his hood!

The 24 went in to pit, but other "dudes" stayed out,
He restarted fourteenth, but at lap 135 is by Riggs for twelfth!

Subway 500

There's a sixth CAUTION a bit later,
Which proved to give the DuPont crew fits!

Some rear lug nuts weren't tightened!
Jeff must return to the pits!

It's the "pits" all right,
Now he's stuck way in the back!

No spot is safe at Martinsville,
But especially where he's at!

He's got 330 laps to make it back to the front!
With aim, sweat and gears,
I'm sure he'll get out of this rut!

We're up to lap 215, and there's a CAUTION for debris!
Jeff won't pit, he stays out
And makes it to fifth with this strategy!

Ya see that?! Just when you think he's *hit the bottom*,
Someone hands him a "shovel!"

He won't let a little setback get him down!
To the front he keeps marching on the double!

Keep that "shovel" handy,
We're gonna need it again!

On lap 257, Jeff's in sixteenth,
But steadily moves forward like I said!

Lap 272 shows him in fifteenth,
Now Kyle Busch is in the lead!

Lap 274 he's in fourteenth,
Then Burton "bangs him" into sixteenth!

The 42 is bouncing back and forth like a "pinball,"
Getting slapped!

Jeff's by Truex then it's Stremme,
Then **full tilt** to Burton's back!

He's finally by Burton
And moves to twelfth position!

Then The 6 spins for a CAUTION,
And we've got us some attrition!

Jeff stays out and restarts fifth!
And advances by Stewart for fourth!

Next by Harvick then Biffle,
For second place, of course!

There are three more CAUTIONS to deal with,
Two of them for Stremme!

My ear bud fell in my coffee cup
As I watched Jeff purpose to fight off Jimmie!

My effort to dry the earpiece
Became a futile attempt!

Don't you know there are holes in there
That are continually leaking wet?!

Subway 500

So with Gevalia dripping down my face,
And Steve and Jeff *bubbling* in my ear,

What we needed was a long GREEN run,
But CAUTION after CAUTION did appear!

So with Jimmie in the lead,
And Jeff hunting down his friend,

With 10 to go, my frantic heart
Watches Newman go by Jeff!

"Help me, doctor!" "I've got a fever and chill!"
"The result of this race is making me ill!"

It's a GREEN/WHITE checker finish,
For the seventh time this year!

The 21st CAUTION in the middle of that,
Popped my hopes right out of gear!

Jeff led the most laps today—168!
420 of the 500 were led by the "HMS Estate!"

Jeff's third place finish was "two little, too late!"
Though Jimmie won today, he didn't seal Jeff's fate!

Jeff's still first in points by a 53-unit margin!
It's off to "Hotlanta" where you know he'll be chargin'!

The battle will continue between Jimmie and Jeff!
For 500 miles I'll attempt to hold my breath!

Four more races left,
If I can keep from having a stroke!

I used to have a handle on life,
But it looks like now it's broke!

But with *Georgia on our mind*,
Let's plan a Victory celebration that's unique——

How 'bout partying in Victory Lane,
With an Atlanta, **flame-broiled** peach!

CHAPTER 33

Pep Boys Auto 500
Atlanta Motor Speedway

October 28, 2007

I wonder how many kids will dress up like Jeff Gordon for Halloween this year? I thought it was cute during today's pre-race show to learn that several years ago Kyle Busch wore a Jeff Gordon costume for Trick-or-Treat! How funny it must be for him today to be Jeff's teammate and be battling him for the championship! Can you imagine?! That's just cool! I wonder if he still has that costume? That would go for top dollar on eBay, I guarantee it! A few years ago, we carved a "Jeff-O-Lantern!" Our traditional fall pumpkin was carved with a big "24" and flames! What we race fans won't do to express ourselves! Today we are commemorating Jeff's fifteenth anniversary! It's here in Atlanta that his Cup career began and Richard Petty's came to a close fifteen years ago. Wow, has a lot happened in fifteen years, or what?! Richard's career ended with a flaming wreck, and the spark of what would become Jeff's future flame-car team was born! Today they gave Jeff the honor of Grand Marshall for the race and he gave the call to "start your engines" from his car! "The king" was given the honor of waving the green flag! Mr. Petty's hat blew off as he was waving the flag, and those of

you who saw it observed a very rare occasion of Richard without a hat on! (Maybe he was giving a "hats off" to Jeff?!) ☺ We also observed a very historical event of two of the greatest stock car drivers that ever lived, being recognized for their incredible accomplishments! Fifteen years and 505 races later, Jeff is charging for his 82nd career win and his fifth Cup Championship!
Who knew?! "You've come a long way, baby!"

Happy Anniversary! Happy Halloween!
Both of these festivities might cause you to scream!

Fifteen short years ago,
Here at this venue in Atlanta,

Started the career of a driver
Who's touted today 'bout as much as Santa!

We've come a long way in 505 races!
It's now the fifth Championship our once-rookie now chases!

Today he's honored with "The king,"
Who on that day, his career ended.

The start of a new icon,
And the close of a legend!

Jeff yelled out the Grand Marshall's call today,
Right from his carbon fiber seat!

While Richard Petty stood atop the stands,
And proudly waved the GREEN!

I wait around like a zombie
For today's very frightful event!

What kind of tricks or treats will erupt,
For our Nextel Cup points-chasing gent?!

The DuPont Chevy has a costume today,
How very apropos!

It's dressed as the *Nicorette Cinnamon Surge Chevy*,
In case you didn't know!

The Newlywed, Biffle sits on the pole,
And from eighth place position, the 24-car will roll!

325 laps is the goal here today!
No clashing with walls or other cars in the way!

So many hair-raising thoughts are haunting our minds!
My soul is filled with unknowns and a chill runs up my spine!

Jimmie Johnson is fearsome!
Intimidating at best!

He lurks around each corner
With the goal of vanquishing our Jeff!

Kurt Busch has been the leader since lap number 2,
Jeff bolts by Kahne for fourth by lap 22!

Some adjustments are made on the 24-machine,
When a blown tire of Juan Pablo brought a CAUTION on 33!

The 8-car had a violation coming into the Pits!
He ran over the cone! A bad deal for him!

Another YELLOW is thrown on lap 39——
Now Jimmie's fourth and Jeff's fifth,
But in this line there's a glitch!

What we need are things to turn around,
And those positions to switch!

Truex took the lead and is having some fun!
After a lap 57 CAUTION, Jeff finds he's bad on short runs!

There are three HMS cars
In third, fourth and fifth!

Jimmie is third, Kyle is fourth,
And next it's Jeff Gordon on the list!

Lap 64 showed the most superlative CAUTION so far today!
So bad, in fact that they RED-flagged this race!

An alarming impact by Mark Martin,
Into the wrecking car of The 38!

As ghastly as it was,
Thankfully all are O.K.!

Jeff's in front of Jimmie for the next several laps!
If I had a magic wand, I'd freeze the race really fast!

The excitement soon perishes,
As does the drive-off in Jeff's car!

There are 6 more laps 'til pit stops,
Which seems so very far!

Pep Boys Auto 500

No need to wait that long!
There's a CAUTION on lap 148!

David Ragan is in the wall,
Due to some fierce blown-tire fate!

Jeff restarts eleventh, The 48 in sixteenth!
Then on 161, Jimmie is by Jeff, which really, really stinks!

That Nicorette Chevy seems smoked!
It's completely out of control!

The calamitous loose conditions,
Are making us Gordon fans watching **choke!**

Jeff hangs around in the late teens,
Hanging on for dear life seemingly for *forever!*

You know his car's really bad,
When being passed by the 55-car
Becomes an easy endeavor!

O.K., there's a CAUTION on 196!
Let's get that heinous machine up on the stick!

We need a *miracle* adjustment to *whip* that car in shape——
Does that mean we need a "miracle whip?!"

Kyle takes the lead on 239,
Jimmie's in third place looking strong and alive!

Then Jeff starts to move!
Like the *Night of the Living Dead!*

242, he's in fifteenth!
245, by Clint for fourteenth!
246, by Newman for thirteenth!

And just like that storybook horseman,
I begin to lose my head!

By lap 265 he's in eleventh!
Then a blasted CAUTION stops this race cold!

It's bad enough that watching NASCAR ages us fans,
But with each caution, I can almost feel myself getting old!

The 24-crew did a great job on that stop!
Jeff is out eighth! (But Jimmie's out in fifth spot!)

A fearsome battle broke out,
As The 24 hunted down The 48!

"Keep your friends close,
And your enemies closer!"—is the saying that "they" say!

What if your enemy is your friend?
Or your friend happens to be your foe?

Just go for the win! Work out the politics later!
Meanwhile, it's a really great show!

(They keep playing the same commercial,
Over and over this day!

I mean, how many times can Jeff go pick up diapers,
In the course of just one race?!)

Speaking of the race!
Jeff's up to seventh, here on lap 294!

By lap 300, it looks like his fuel
Is just about a half a lap too short!

There's a big debate on lap 318's CAUTION,
Jeff's got a vibration, and four tires would be awesome!

But track position is crucial!
Oh my stars! Just what to do?!

Four tires and fuel it is!
Great job by the 24-crew!

The leader when we restart is Car Number 11.
Who stayed out which was really quite a risky decision!

When you're that low on gas,
And your tires are bald,

Your chances are slim, buddy,
Do you want your machine to stall?!

Jeff's plan is to "blow right by" the guys in front of him,
Though he's currently back in eleventh!

With four fresh tires and fuel to finish,
Let's get that motor revvin'!

Just when you think a miracle will prevail,
Something lousy happens to suck the wind from your sails!

Right at the re-start, Hamlin's out of gas!
He doesn't move forward and Truex is hard in his back!

Jimmie goes around that mess
And claims the first position!

Jeff's up to ninth at the restart
Due to that little attrition!

ANOTHER GREEN, WHITE checker finish?
It's become the norm this crazy year!

And just as we're ready to move forward again,
Something happens that's really queer!

Dale Jr.'s wheel decided to come off,
And so therein ends the race!

This must be a joke! The 48 wins again?
There must be some mistake!

I know it seems like I'm in denial,
But trust me, **I'm really not!**

But are you SURE this race is over,
And Jeff's not the winner, but ends in seventh spot?

Now, seventh isn't bad,
But the fact that Jimmie won is killer!

Jeff still has the points lead, but only by 9!
And you thought *Amityville Horror* was a chiller?!

This Chase is terrifyingly close!
With the shocking turns of events!

We know our driver and team can tough it out!
But can his fans handle all the suspense?!

Pep Boys Auto 500

Pull up your bootstraps!
Strap on your spurs!

Let's ride on into Texas,
Where to Victory Lane we'll surge!

Now's a perfect time to end the winless streak there!
And closer to that Cup to vehemently draw near!

Shake the dust off!
This Atlanta race is DONE!

We'll move on to bigger and better things,
There's a Texas race to be WON!

POINT STANDINGS:

1.	Jeff Gordon	6201	Leader
2.	Jimmie Johnson	6192	-9
3.	Clint Bowyer	6090	-111
4.	Carl Edwards	5940	-261
5.	Tony Stewart	5879	-322
6.	Kyle Busch	5873	-328
7.	Kevin Harvick	5809	-392
8.	Jeff Burton	5801	-400
9.	Kurt Busch	5782	-419
10.	Denny Hamlin	5777	-424
11.	Matt Kenseth	5753	-448
12.	Martin Truex Jr.	5688	-513

CHAPTER 34

Dickies 500
Texas Motor Speedway

November 4, 2007

*T*oday started out **extremely exciting!** You see, it was 60 de-grees outside when I woke up this morning! If you just said to yourself, "Big deal!" then you must not be living in south Florida like I am! Any little bit of refreshing, non-humidity-filled, sweltering, 90-degree air does wonders for your outlook on life! For one thing, you are immediately psyched-out into thinking: "It must be fall!" If you live in the north somewhere, I'll bet you never give it a thought how very exciting it is for us southern folk to be able to wear long sleeves! . . . And be able to dig out our homemade beef stew and pumpkin apple streusel muffin recipes!! . . . And have an excuse to buy cider and donuts at the grocery store! (You also know it's fall by gaining an extra 10 lbs. without even thinking about it!) It **only** got up to 80 degrees today! But it was a "cool" 80 degrees! (I promise!) A light breeze, no humidity and just perfect! Being that the race started later today, I even took a 20-minute nap out on our trampoline be-fore the race! It was so nice to get a break from my four walls and this computer! It was a great day, and I had a good "vibe" about the race today! I just knew Jeff was going to slay that Texas track and

*leave with a win and a padded points-lead! Well, just as my husband "almost" slayed the coral snake that was on our porch this past Friday, the win, as well as the snake, slipped through the cracks! But, I have not given up on Jeff and Team 24! **No way!** We have two more races to "get it done!" It's not over 'til it's over, and I haven't heard any "rotund effeminate being" singing yet! Perhaps my "good vibe" was meant for next week! You just wait! There'll be some "snake slaying" at Phoenix, for sure! Go get 'em, Jeff! Meanwhile, I heard we are getting another cool front on Wednesday! It's a good thing!*
It will help me with this temporary meltdown
I'm having after today's race!

Jeff moseyed on into Texas,
And he surely had somethin' to prove!

But there's a target on his back,
The manhunt is on!
There's a gun slingin' bandit on the move!

The bandit's branded with a "48" on his stern,
He's a tough one, of that there's no doubt!

Jeff starts in second place, all armed and ready,
For the showdown between his "pardner" and himself!

Tensions are high and mounting by the nano-second!
The air is thick with pure sweat!

The showdown starts here, at Texas Motor Speedway,
Who'll come out on top as Best of the Best?!

The 24 must be on guard,
Watch his back every minute,

Dickies 500

Because if there's trouble on the "range",
He doesn't want to be in it!

If pressure creates diamonds, Jeff's holding a 24-karat!
——To be revealed at the most opportune time!

A couple more weeks, to rub off some rough,
And reveal an entire diamond mine!

Time to get this show on, and warm up those "horses!"
There's a long, hot battle ahead!

I've said it before and I'll say it again,
A lesser man would be dead!

Little Ella was with her parents
For all of the pre-race thrills!

Nestled snug in Daddy's arms,
Looking cool, calm and chilled!

Four F-16's screamed loudly overhead,
As Ingrid covered her delicate ears——

She's getting used to this stuff, safe with Mom and Dad,
She realizes there's no need to fear!

With a kiss "goodbye" to Daddy,
Who will soon be *Gone With the Wind!*

She looks forward to the day
When she can whisper in his ear,

"Come on Daddy,
Go for the win!"

So with the Grand Marshall's call
From the Dallas Maverick's Dirk Nowitzki,
190,000 fans are on their feet!

500 miles at this grueling place,
Would make any cowboy weak in his knees!

Jeff struggles right away and slips to sixth spot,
And we're only on the 2nd measly lap!

Our pole-sitter, Truex, leads the first 6,
Then he and Montoya traded positions on the track!

Lap 9 it began, the "cat and mouse" game,
Between Jeff and Jimmie—a.k.a., "Jesse" James!

—NASCAR'S own "American Outlaw,"
Stealing points and wins from our driver,
On every Wanted *poster is written his name!*

Back to reality here, we're on lap 14,
And already, the CAUTION flag waves!

Time to run in for adjustments and only two tires,
Jeff's in first when the GREEN again waves!

There's "YELLOW fever" all over, in these here parts,
The fourth CAUTION came on lap 35!

Jeff stayed out in the lead,
Jimmie pit and is in 30th,
Too bad this isn't the way it ended here tonight!

Kyle took the point on lap 46,
Jeff's falling every few laps or so—

Dickies 500

On lap 72 he was in sixth but pits on GREEN,
He's a lap down and in 38th and my innerds *start to scream!*

We hold our breath for a while, hoping for no Cautions!
——No need to add insult to injury here today!

Then on lap 92, Jeff gets his lead back,
Thanks to a full cycle of stops during the GREEN flag!

He's in fourth on 93, then seventh on 101,
And realizing The 48 is right behind him isn't any fun!

Like a stampede of confused cattle,
On lap 131, a big wreck for the sixth CAUTION wipes out
more than one!

Stremme had a rear tire go down,
And collected The 21 and The 45!

Jeff pits and returns in fifteenth,
While Jimmie Johnson came out ninth!

On 152, Kasey Kahne had a tire issue,
And into the pits he goes!

The 48 is in eighth, and Jeff's in fifteenth——
What ails his car?! Nobody seems to know!

Jeff goes to tenth on lap 185,
Then seventh on lap 189.

Allmendinger has had so many problems today,
That Red Bull car must be marked with a BULL'S EYE!

After A.J.'s CAUTION on 212,
There's a HUGE wreck on 219!

Collecting multiple cars in the way!
Jeff had just passed The 25 (who was the cause of this thing)
And just in time had a narrow escape!

Another CAUTION on 232,
Greg Biffle took a turn-4 spin!

Time to free up The 24
And help the shape that it's in!

Jeff exits seventh, Jimmie's in third!
His points are waning today, and it's simply absurd!

Lap 247 reveals a bad thing.
Jeff's the slowest car of the top fourteen!

"The worst I've been all day!"
I heard him say the next lap!

Someone wake me from this nightmare!
Please give me a slap!

Maybe Steve should call DuPont Performance Alliance,
Or visit PA24.com!

Someone out there must be able to help,
And figure out just what's going on!

Hamlin and Kenseth battle for the lead,
Denny wins out, but Jeff's in thirteenth!

Dickies 500

Which isn't too horrible considering all in the pack,
But it's a major problem with only 15 cars on the lead lap!

The thing that's so nauseating
Is that Jimmie's in second!

—Until he takes the lead on 272
When the CAUTION is for Hamlin and Matt Kenseth!

But Jimmie's lead was short-lived,
As Kyle took it away.
Now Jeff's in eleventh on lap 278!

The car's finally the best it's been
On lap 289!

Which frequently seems to happen
When we're about out of time!

The last CAUTION of the day happens on lap 298!
Biffle's car is on fire and has definitely seen its fate!

Jeff goes and gets four tires on this Caution of late!
He's out tenth . . .

. . . But how is Kurt in sixth position
When he's had problems all day?!

It's lap 317, and Jeff's up to seventh,
Which any other day would be FAB!

But Jimmie and Kenseth
Are having a massive battle for FIRST!

And the points that Jeff could lose . . .
This is really BAD!

With 2 laps to go,
"Mr. James" stole the lead!

Jeff's in seventh——
Same finishes those two guys just had last week!

I can't believe Johnson won again!
I'm so mad I could just eat sand!

Snake-bit again!
It's time The 24 resumed the upper hand!

Jeff's now second in points!
Thirty from Jimmie's back!

I do believe, son,
At this moment we've been had!

Wyatt Earp would be proud
Of this grand-theft display!

Who stole the "horses"
That should have been under Jeff's hood today?

I feel like someone shoved me into the nearest Texas cactus!
There's only two weeks left to improve on our tactics!

Let's give Jeff *a fresh horse* as we head out to Phoenix!
Let his finish be jubilant! One that won't require Kleenex!

All is not lost!
We'll get that Phoenix win!

Now lets "get on our horsies
And ride on outta here, Pilgrim!"

POINT STANDING:

1.	Jimmie Johnson	6382	Leader
2.	Jeff Gordon	6352	-30
3.	Clint Bowyer	6201	-181
4.	Kyle Busch	6043	-339
5.	Carl Edwards	6025	-357
6.	Tony Stewart	6009	-373
7.	Jeff Burton	5951	-431
8.	Kevin Harvick	5943	-439
9.	Kurt Busch	5929	-453
10.	Matt Kenseth	5928	-454
11.	Denny Hamlin	5858	-524
12.	Martin Truex Jr.	5858	-524

CHAPTER 35

Checker Auto Parts 500
presented by Pennzoil
Phoenix International Raceway

November 11, 2007

I haven't felt such intense, peevish indignation like I am feeling right now, in a long time! After the Checker Auto Parts 500, I felt as though my burning face may combust and set my entire home on fire! I couldn't hold back the hot "lava" from my eyes no matter how hard I tried! I am still finding it difficult to speak this morning-after as I write this! Do I take these races too seriously? You better believe it! Sorry, I just can't help it! If Jeff loses this Championship, to me, it will be extremely "unjust." Not that we didn't all know the rules going into this thing, but the whole Chase format is ridiculously unjust! The fact that Jeff may be gypped out of another Championship since this Chase format started, just because someone wanted to get more television viewership really does not sit well with me! The man has earned the overall most points! He should win it! Period! Why has Jeff's car been so sub-par these past couple of weeks? What is the reason for this? Let me tell you, "Inquiring minds want to know!" I wasn't even going to write a re-cap for this race. I was going to scrap the whole book thing altogether. At this point, I am so burned out and frustrated for many reasons, I WANT to give up! But, unfortunately for me, that is not in my nature. "The show must go on," God is still on His throne, and it will be a growing experience for me to try and write a re-cap for this race when frankly, I don't want to! Besides, anything can happen! Jeff can still walk away with the Championship, although in his post-race interview, it sounded like he has given up. **Well let me tell you something Jeff, your fans haven't given up on you!** You can still do this! It's all about attitude and determination! I love the little story that tells about a woman who woke up with only three hairs left on her head. She happily said, hmm, I think I'll braid my hair today! And so with the three hairs, she did and went on to have a wonderful day. The next day, she woke up and only had two hairs left. "I think I'll part my hair down the middle today and wear it that way!" Again, she had a wonderful day with her new hairstyle. The next morning she woke up and there was only one hair left on her head! "Oh, good!" she said, "I get to put my hair in a pony tail today!" Happy as a lark, she did just that and had a fabulous day! Well, the next morning she woke up and she was completely bald! You know what she said? "Thank goodness I don't have to do my hair today!" Now that's what I call positive thinking! Miracles happen every day! Haven't you ever seen the movie, "Facing the Giants?" Well if you haven't, you should! Jeff is facing a "giant" this coming Sunday, but it CAN be overcome! Never give up! Never lose faith! Go get 'em, Jeff! Your fans are counting on you and beyond that, we **KNOW** you can do it!!!! I'd like to end with a great quote by Lance Armstrong, that has encouraged me personally:

**"Pain is temporary. It may last a minute, or an hour,
or a day, or a year, but eventually it will subside
and something else will take its place.
If I quit, however, it lasts forever."**

The *thirst* is overwhelming,
In the desert here, today.

Checker Auto Parts 500

Every corpuscle jammed inside of our veins
Is parched and begging for grace!

There's such a short time——
Only 312 laps——
To try and gain ground at this flat 1-mile track!

Should be easy for our guy,
He won here in the spring!

But like a bad, itchy rash,
The 48 pricks ferocious sting!

Carl Edwards won the pole——
No back flips for that!

He's just happy to make the Bud Shootout,
And to be where he's at!

Jeff qualified third, and so far, it's looking good!
But the true test will be shown
When we see what's under that hood!

Johnson sniffs closely, beginning in sixth,
But our goal for today is for his points-lead to nix!

But before the on-track action,
Once again we are blessed,

By Dr. Jesse McGuire's Anthem playing,
On his silver trumpet with finesse!

After the fireworks, the engines ignite!
Let's *get this party started*, we're ready to fight!

Johnson started sixth,
But moves to fifth the 1st lap

He's like trying to ward off a fungus . . .
You think it's gone, then it's back!

Jimmie's *sniffing* Jeff's bumper by only lap 5!
Jeff divulges his car's real loose, while The 48's on the fly!

Why does this so frequently happen?
Who puts these cars together?

Seems like lately The 48 is strong and healthy,
While The 24 remains "under the weather!"

While Jeff nurtures his "buggy,"
Jimmie passes him clean.

The CAUTION's out on lap 25,
Time to help that DuPont machine!

We're up to lap 53; Jeff passed Newman for fourth!
Jeff stated he's still struggling,
But his Chevy's better than before!

Our hopes rise up high!
Lap 70 we're slightly elated!

"It's better!" "It's better!"
"It's not bad right now!" Jeff stated!

——Must be good on the long-runs,
Let's keep it going, *for Pete's sake!*

I've heard about all the "loose conditions"
My feeble mind can take!

After a lap 86 CAUTION for debris,
And another on 96 for a wreck——
(Stewart gave Nemecheck a significantly hard deck!)

Jeff's in sixth by lap 103,
But boxed in by The 2 and The 12!

If those guys would just **MOVE**,
It would be really, really *swell!*

Robby Gordon's been fighting hard
To get the lap he lost back!

He doesn't seem to care who's in his way!
Not even our championship-hunting Champ!

Carl Edwards' engine is blowing on lap 106,
The CAUTION is thrown, is this something that can be fixed?

Thank goodness The 7 was the "lucky dog!"
Now he'll be out of everyone's way!

Jeff stayed out at this Caution and is fourth,
——But on a troubling note, Jimmie's in second place!

Dale Jr. got loose on the exit of turn 2.
The CAUTION's out and now on that Impala,
There's some minor work to do!

Jeff pit for adjustments, while Johnson stayed out.
Now Jeff's in fifteenth, but will be good when
The next Caution comes out!

Meanwhile he's mired midst a whacky, nervous wad!
Lap 128 he panics, thinking his right rear felt low and odd!

The next CAUTION's for the "newbie" of Jacques Villeneuve,
He found when you're pinched into the wall,
That thing *ain't* gonna move!

Jeff's out of that "wad" and in fourth, just as planned!
But The 48's in tenth place——not far enough in the back!

CAUTION number seven for The 9 in the wall,
Jeff's in third, Jimmie's in sixth,
Right where we started this brawl!

Jeff's up to second on lap 159!
Screams for clean air and bonus points,
Has us all out of our minds!

It's lap 173 and Jeff's tires are fried, used-up and spent!
So he must pit under GREEN
Which has me out of shape and bent!

Now he's in 26th and 1 lap down!
Over and again he and Biffle swap positions——
The 16 is driving like a clown!

Then in the blink of an eye, The 48 pits!
Jeff's immediately up to second!
——Could we make one position better than this?!

Blaney spun out on lap 233,
After stops, Jeff's eighth and Ryan Newman leads.

Next in line it's Matt Kenseth, then Stewart,
Then Bowyer. Truex in fifth,
Round the current top-five warriors.

Johnson's in sixth,
Jeff's mediocre in eighth——

Can't we please mend that Impala?
It's really getting late!

Nemecheck wrecks again,
For the lap 243 CAUTION.

As laps wane down,
I'm getting increasingly nauseous!

Harvick's racing Jeff hard,
The nerve of that guy!

He has contact with Jeff
And left a tire-rub on his side!

Frustration mounts with only 38 laps to go!
The 48 is second, Jeff's twelfth!
How does this happen? Does anyone know?

There's a wicked battle for first
Between Kenseth and The 48!

My heart turns evil——
Hoping Jimmie wrecks at this stage in the game!

But no, his car's *perfect*,
Which allows him to take the lead!

While Jeff's hanging in tenth,
Praying earnestly for some speed!

Then suddenly I was jolted
Almost out of my chair!

Did I just hear there are only 6 laps left,
From that guy on the air?!

This just can't be true!
Who warped the time?!

I thought surely I heard wrong!
Please say it's a lie!

This just can't be happening!
Does The 48 think he's Jeff?

Winning four weeks in a row?
Right at the Chase end?

Someone wake me up!
I'm having a terrible nightmare!

Did I just see Johnson win again?
This bad dream really has me scared!

I felt like someone sucked the wind,
Completely out of my lungs!

I felt like imploding and exploding all at once,
There was just nowhere I could run!

It was true! It happened!
And Jeff ended up tenth!

Checker Auto Parts 500

I wasn't sure who to be mad at,
But my feelings sure were intense!

One week left to go,
And now Jeff's 86 points behind!

It seems like *Mission Impossible,*
But there's no way 24-fans will give up on their guy!

Who unleashed this deadly *virus*
On the DuPont Chevy these past few weeks?

Where's the antidote when you need it?
Do you suppose too soon, he peaked?

No! Not true!
Jeff's whole season has been at the top!

Consistent and valiant,
Even after his 300-plus points were hocked!

Right now I'm going to go sip on a fire extinguisher,
And try not to lose my head!

It's not over yet, people!
The Drive for Five is not dead!

Miracles happen every day!
Perhaps God has one waiting up His sleeve!

And is waiting for just the right time down at Homestead,
To let His power unleash!

We'll just have to wait,
Nothing we can do about it now.

But painfully endure this next week,
Wondering,
Will we rise to Victory, or have to extend a humble bow?

So, come on 24-team!
The south awaits your skill!

Work 'round the clock to install some magic,
Right now there's no time to kill!

We're counting on you!
Don't throw in the towel just yet!

You've already got the world's best driver!
Just give him a car that will soar like a jet!

POINT STANDINGS:

RANK	DRIVER	BEHIND
1	Jimmie Johnson	Leader
2	Jeff Gordon	-86
3	Clint Bowyer	-241
4	Kyle Busch	-387
5	Tony Stewart	-403
6	Matt Kenseth	-469
7	Kevin Harvick	-479
8	Jeff Burton	-483
9	Carl Edwards	-505
10	Kurt Busch	-516
11	Martin Truex Jr.	-563
12	Denny Hamlin	-599

CHAPTER 36

Ford 400
Homestead-Miami Speedway

November 18, 2007

Well, here we are. What a season this was! This re-cap pretty much sums up my feelings, especially at the end, so I won't elaborate here. But I want to thank all of my faithful readers on the Jeff Gordon Network each week. Your encouragement kept me going, and I hope it's been fun and refreshing for you to read this style of re-cap! I don't know if I will do this again next year. Time will tell, but it's been fun for me too! Regardless of the season's outcome, we have so very much to be thankful for! One thing I am thankful for is that we haven't had a hurricane this year! After going through three direct hits in a row and having to put a new roof on our house, trust me, I'm beyond thankful for no hurricanes this season! (Although I'm feeling quite winded after this NASCAR season!) ☺ I wish everyone a wonderful off-season and holiday time! Only around 90 more days until Daytona! Woo Hoo!!! Don't forget to count your blessings . . . we all have many! Until next season,
God bless!

Anyway you slice it, it's a historical day!
The final drive for the *current car* before it's auctioned away!

Ricky Rudd's final race after 906!
Having Johnson in the lead is something we need to fix!

Can Jeff make the record of 30 top tens in a season?
Are you kidding? He's used to setting records,
For him it should be easy!

The last race is here. The final chapter will be written.
2007 has been an incredible year!
We've been blessed more than we've been bitten!

The off-season awaits us; tomorrow the countdown begins!
We'll start checking off on our calendars
'Til that month the Daytona 500 is in!

But today we close the books,
On the 2007 NASCAR Nextel Cup season,

Down in warm, beautiful south Florida!
(Did you think I lived here without a reason?!)

Regardless of the outcome,
Rick Hendrick earns his seventh Cup!

Such an amazing man and organization!
To his example, we can all look up!

The teams love him like a dad,
With grace and character he leads!

On top of all that,
He produces some cool cars with incredible speeds!

Ford 400

Today the battle continues,
Between those top two HMS teammates!

Who will clinch the title?
Who will end in second place?

At today's Ford 400,
Appropriately, Mr. Edsel Ford Grand Marshall's today!

I've been over-anxious all day,
And ready to get this race underway!

Greg Biffle will shoot to win again here,
As he's done the past three years!

Can Jeff overcome his 86-point deficit,
And calm down all of our fears?

In four races this season,
He's gained more than 100 points on The 48!

So we know it can be done!
But for now we'll hope and wait!

As if the agony needed to be prolonged—
Jimmie's on the pole!

Although Jeff starts off this race in eleventh,
That top spot is his goal!

Johnson claims five bonus points,
Right away, for leading a lap.

Then Newman's heist of first position,
Puts Johnson two spots back!

Jeff begins advancing, immediately if not sooner!
By lap 8 he's swapping positions eight and nine
With Tony Stewart!

He states he's "awfully good,
Just a little tight in the middle!"

Is it possible he's got a car today
That might be "fit as a fiddle?"

By lap 24, The 24's in fifth!
But on lap 27, Truex goes by him!

Lap 42 shows Johnson, in seventh, right behind Jeff!
This battle rages on, and it will be agonizing to the end!

GREEN pit stops begin, and Jeff goes in on lap 50.
Just at the wrong time, The 8 brings out a CAUTION,
And it's here we get real "iffy!"

——Will Jeff be a lap down, or just at the tail end?
NASCAR is figuring it out!
On this issue, a few minutes they'll spend!

Apparently Jeff and Jimmie
will now be at the tail end of the line!
The 48's in eighteenth and Jeff's in nineteenth right behind!

Then just as we go GREEN, Jr. takes a spin!
The 31 got into him, and we have a CAUTION once again!

Many ran over some metal debris,
And one of the many was Jeff!

Ford 400

He'll dive into the Pits for right sides and fuel——
Better to be safe than end in a wreck!

On lap 63 when the GREEN flag waves once more,
The 48's in 22nd and in 20th is The 24!

Jeff starts to fly through the field,
Checking off positions right and left!

He's up to thirteenth on lap 72,
When the CAUTION flag waves again!

Menard got loose and lost it,
Driving hard out of turn 4,

Then Steve has a plan for position——
They'll take two tires instead of four!

So Jeff pit for right sides only!
He's back out on the track and in **third!**

Johnson's in seventeenth, mired in traffic!
"Anything can happen here!"
——Said the voice in my head that I heard!

I'm ashamed to admit the evil thoughts I was having——
Wishing ill fate on the competition!

I don't yearn for any harm on anyone in the field!
But I sure would welcome some attrition!

Jeff's still in third, with Kenseth right behind!
If The 24 could just go get those five bonus points,
Before Matt once again rockets by!

Well, *fat chance*, it didn't happen,
Matt's by him on lap 82!

Then Matt re-claimed the lead,
Just like I knew that he would do!

Well, the 2-tire deal was only a temporary fix!
Jeff's in eighth falling back to Jimmie's nose . . .
——Wouldn't you know it would be his!

Lap 111 and The 24 is still a little bit too tight!
But he continues working hard! Never giving up the fight!

Jeff and Jimmie pit on GREEN at lap 130!
Jeff beat The 48 off Pit road!
Looks like the 24-pit crew sure did hurry!

Lap 149 proves Jeff abducted sixth from Stewart!
Then Newman spun out, right in front of Jeff!
Thankfully, he made it through it!

Time for Jeff to go in,
On this fourth CAUTION of the day,

He "fish-tails" out of his pit,
Trying to stay clear of other cars in the way!

He's out in a good spot, in position number five!
Then another CAUTION on 158; Jeff's staying out this time!

Hamlin took the lead on lap 166,
Shortly after Jeff took third and is getting closer to him!

Ford 400

Sam Hornish, Jr. is too high and scrapes the wall!
Another CAUTION on 192! Jeff's out fourth, Jimmie's sixth——
Can't that guy's positions ever fall?!

Around lap 208, Jeff waffles between second and third!
Lap 210, he's running faster than the leader!
I was so excited about what I just heard!

Time is running out, my hopes are sinking fast!
It's times like this you wish
The HMS motor on The 48 just wouldn't last!

After lap 242's GREEN pit, Jeff's still plowin' like crazy!
He's giving it all he's got, showing regardless of the car,
He's sure not lazy!

With only 14 laps to go, The 20 is backwards into the wall!
You guessed it, another CAUTION,
And The 17 still leads them all!

Counting down the laps,
My sadness begins to well up.

Doesn't look like this is the year,
For our Champ to get his fifth cup!

Kenseth takes the win for this race,
And does double burnouts with Jimmie.

Jeff ends on a strong note in fourth position,
Jimmie in seventh, but the **"whole thing"** he's winning.

I personally feel like I've been hit by a truck!
So exhausted from this roller coaster,
That to the seats I've been stuck!

I have so many questions that I just don't understand,
But I have to trust the One who holds it all in His hands!

I'm going to keep a stiff upper lip,
And follow the example of Jeff and the 24-men!

Congratulations to The 48-team,
And to the stellar job they pulled off at the end!

I'm continually amazed at Jeff
And the fetes this year he's pulled off!

But the biggest, by far,
Is the class he displayed through it all!

You know he was hurting, you could see it in his face!
But keeps that award-winning smile with style and grace!

But being Thanksgiving week,
He surely has blessings to count!

He was dominant all year!
And broke records all around!

Then add to the fact that in 36 race begins,
He has 21 top fives and 30 top tens!
And, oh, 7 poles and 6 amazing wins!

He out-scored The 48 in 22 of those races!
Consistent all year long, keeping up with their paces!

But Jeff, we wish you some rest
And precious times with your "fam,"

Ford 400

Special moments with Ingrid and Ella
And the rest of your clan.

You've earned a break, and your fans want you to know,
We are **SO VERY PROUD** of you,
More than we could ever show!

Our torch for you keeps burning, and for Cup number 5!
Get rested up and ready to come back
Looking strong and alive!

Thanks for the great moments in 2007!
I can't believe the last chapter of this season has ended!

I wish all of you 24-fans a fantastic holiday season!
The comradery we share goes without reason!

If you see a fellow 24-fan walking down the street,
Don't forget to high-five them, or give a special greet!

You can spot us a mile away,
We're the ones going bald or gray!

We'll probably talk with a stutter,
Or have a nervous tic that just won't go away!

We won't have any fingernails,
We'll probably be talking out loud to ourselves!

And at this point, we're covered in wrinkles,
Looking old and in poor health!

But we'll sacrifice our bodies, our minds and our wit!
We'll wear our 24-shirt until it no longer fits!

We're not as dumb as we look!
You can count on that!

Regardless of ridiculous points formats,
WE KNOW, JEFF, YOU'RE THE CHAMP!!!!!!!!!

Rank	Driver	Behind	Starts	Poles	Wins	Top 5	Top 10
1	Jimmie Johnson	Leader	36	4	10	20	24
2	Jeff Gordon	-77	36	7	6	21	30
3	Clint Bowyer	-346	36	2	1	5	17
4	Matt Kenseth	-425	36	0	2	13	22
5	Kyle Busch	-430	36	0	1	11	20
6	Tony Stewart	-481	36	0	3	11	23
7	Kurt Busch	-492	36	1	2	6	14
8	Jeff Burton	-492	36	0	1	9	18
9	Carl Edwards	-501	36	1	3	11	15
10	Kevin Harvick	-524	36	0	1	4	15
11	Martin Truex Jr.	-559	36	1	1	7	14
12	Denny Hamlin	-580	36	1	1	12	18

CHAPTER 37

The Many Emotions of a
Jeff Gordon Fan

by Maria Bennett

*T*his was the very first Jeff Gordon poem I ever wrote, probably three or four years ago. (I updated the crew chief to present day.) This is the poem that gave me the idea of possibly doing an entire season's-worth of race re-caps in lyrical style. I put off trying to write the re-caps until 2007. Once I started, I was determined to finish or die trying! If nothing else, I proved to myself that it could indeed be done!

I hope you've enjoyed my "personal test!"

'Twas the night before race day, and all through our house,
All the creatures are stirring, as the excitement mounts!

You see, Gordon fans we are, and mighty proud of it!
All donned in 24-garb, oh how we love it!

Oh, we're not obsessed, only slightly crazed!
We watch him time and again, and we're simply amazed!

That 24-car is all shiny and slick!
Get the tire pressures right so that Baby will stick!

Whether he starts on the pole, or the middle or rear,
If he's in your rearview mirror, you've got reason to fear!

The team has worked hard, Stevie's been up all night,
To get the right set-up, to not be loose or too tight!

As he flies down the straight-a-way,
Those awesome flames are a blur!

Jeff starts to lap the field,
Which always causes quite a stir!

"Git'er done, Jeff!" We're all yelling out loud!
You're alone, out in front, no other cars are around!

"CAUTION'S OUT!" Yells "D.W.", as the cars all take heed,
A wreck in turn two, there goes Jeff's 3-second lead!

No one's hurt, thank the Lord, as we pray them all through!
Now Steve's got the task of figuring out what to do——

Come in or stay out? Scuff tires or *stickers*?
Decisions like that would make me even sicker!

My stomach's in knots, my nails are all bit!
My nerves are now shot, now that Jeff has to pit!

Track-bar adjustment, wedge in or wedge out?
He knows what is needed to keep that car stout!

Maybe gas and go to keep that great lead!
Come on pit-crew, give him just what he needs!

The Many Emotions of a Jeff Gordon Fan

It's very stressful to watch NASCAR,
BUT WOULD BE MORE STRESSFUL TO NOT!

We cheer our Jeff on,
Because we love him a lot!

So we'll put up with the ulcers and increasing gray hair,
And the calls that are made that don't always seem fair!

When he goes for the win,
That RUSH is overwhelming!

Turn your cameras on, folks,
It's time to start filming!

There he goes to the front, to win AGAIN,
Can you believe it?!

To the checkered flag he goes
To pledge his allegiance!

Thanks, Jeff, for the excitement that you bring to race day!
It's because of you, that we fans just can't stay away!

We will stand by you, through thick or through thin!
Whether you end up in the back or go for the win!

We're your dedicated friends and fans to the end!
"We're there for you, Man!" On this you can depend!

No matter the "Young Guns," "Old Guns," or the rest,
The World's Greatest Driver is YOU,
YOU'RE THE BEST!

~Blessed are the cracked, for they
Are the ones who let in the light!~

ABOUT THE AUTHOR

Maria Bennett is a wife, home school mom, singer, songwriter, recording artist, author, and speaker, residing in Palm Beach County, FL, with her husband, Marty, and their son, Anthony. Marty and Maria are originally from up-state New York, but have lived in south Florida for their entire 23 years of marriage.

Maria has had the privilege of singing a duet with Dove and Grammy award winner, Larnell Harris, in concert.

She has presented concerts for many churches, Christian schools, and seminars for many years.

She is also frequently invited to sing her rendition of our National Anthem, and has sung for countless professional sporting and civic events, as well as the opening of a Ricky VanShelton, Daryl Singletary concert.

Maria also presented a Patriotic mini-concert for Jeff Gordon and the fans at his fan club event at Daytona USA, Daytona Beach, FL.

Besides singing and writing, one of Maria's great loves is the sport of NASCAR! With the release of this, her first book, she has combined her love of writing with her love of NASCAR.

Maria has also written and recorded the CD single, "Overwhelmed" created for Jeff Gordon and his wife Ingrid, in honor of their first-born child, Ella Sofia.

For more information, please visit:
www.TheOriginalRoute66.com.

Printed in the United States
201069BV00004B/1-99/A